THE BORDER WITHIN

THE BORDER WITHIN

Vietnamese Migrants Transforming
Ethnic Nationalism in Berlin

PHI HONG SU

To Minh and Freddy,

With thanks for following along with this book's protagonists
as they rebuild their lives after war and border crossings.

Much appreciated,
Phi

Williamstown, MA
July 2022

STANFORD UNIVERSITY PRESS
Stanford, California

STANFORD UNIVERSITY PRESS
Stanford, California

©2022 by Phi Hong Su. All rights reserved.

No part of this book may be reproduced or transmitted in any form or by any means, electronic or mechanical, including photocopying and recording, or in any information storage or retrieval system without the prior written permission of Stanford University Press.

Printed in the United States of America on acid-free, archival-quality paper

Library of Congress Cataloging-in-Publication Data available upon request.

ISBN 9781503630062 (cloth)
ISBN 9781503630147 (paperback)
ISBN 9781503630154 (electronic)

Cover photo: Berlin Raoul-Wallenberg-Straße. Claire Greenstein.

Cover design: Rob Ehle

Typeset by Kevin Barrett Kane in 10/14 Minion Pro

Cho ba mẹ

Contents

Preface

The Vietnamese language was the last thing my sister, Phung, and I expected to miss during our high school study abroad in Germany. Like other children of working-class immigrants and refugees in our Southern California suburb, my sister and I spoke elementary Vietnamese at home. We translated as best we could for our monolingual parents at medical and welfare offices. In fact, we associated our heritage language with this burden of cultural brokering. But the German language and our brief study abroad offered something entirely different. Our stay with our host families in the town of Gummersbach allowed us to peer into an alternative upbringing, where members of a household and community communicated fluently in the same tongue. Parents could navigate the society in which they lived and therefore trusted their children to attend parties and walk around at night without fear of an unknown milieu. At fifteen, I saw the German and Vietnamese languages as representing forking paths: expanding versus constricting horizons, freedom versus captivity.

But after two weeks of speaking only English or faltering German with our host families, something odd happened. Strolling down the street on a day trip to Bonn, my sister and I paused at the sound of that familiar yet unexpected language, dancing with its six tones. Our eyes hunted for the source: an Asian woman clad in a thick autumn jacket, calling after a child who was scuttling about on the cobblestone streets. Phung eagerly accosted the woman to ask, "Auntie, are you Vietnamese?"[1] The woman's affirmative response and our brief exchange have been blurred by the intervening seventeen years since. My sister insists I quipped something to the effect of, "We're in Europe, and the first thing you get excited about is talking Vietnamese?" This snapshot surges back when I think of how people "perceive their national identities as real, tangible and meaningful pillars of [their] selfhood."[2]

I unwittingly carried this interest in ethnic nationhood with me into undergraduate studies, when my keenness to soak up Marx alarmed my father, a former officer in the Army of the Republic of (South) Vietnam. After the communist victory over the South in 1975, he languished for eight years in so-called reeducation camp—a political prison. My strangely charged conversation with my father echoed yet another thread of Cold War politics I saw brewing within a presumably unified "ethnic community." In 2009, onlookers became incensed by an art exhibit hosted by the Vietnamese American Arts and Letters Association (VAALA) in Little Saigon, California. Demonstrators vandalized and successfully shut down the art exhibit that had included a photograph of a woman donning the red Vietnamese flag with a yellow star and sitting next to a bust of communist leader Hồ Chí Minh. Never mind that the artist intended his work as commentary on the ironic commodification of communism in postwar Vietnam.[3] In the following years, I came to organize with and study VAALA members. I heard at length about how the art exhibit curators endured threats of violence as well as verbal and physical attacks during the protests. But although the protesters identified themselves as anticommunist, the Vietnamese coethnics who were the object of their scorn did not correspondingly identify as communist. Many VAALA members were, like the protesters, refugees or the children of refugees. Most were critical of the Vietnamese government. Yet fear of provoking anticommunists and of disrespecting "our elders" nevertheless informed how we went about organizing an upcoming film festival. The prospect of anticommunist protests presented itself everywhere, though self-identified communists were nowhere to be found.

In time, I came to see migrant anticommunism as revealing a more universal truth: state formation in a homeland, and subsequent emigration out of it, transform ethnonational identities in durable ways. Like Cubans and other Cold War migrants to the United States, Vietnamese Americans intuited that certain images, references, and ideologies were simply unacceptable. The 1.5- and second-generation VAALA organizers like me discerned these often implicit rubrics even though few of us had ever spoken with our parents about the war.[4] Instead, we learned these lessons through strained conversations— conversations about reading Marx as sociology majors or wanting to visit Vietnam. We learned through subconsciously mirroring the frowns on other people's faces as they discussed their fears of anti-communist backlash. We learned through organizing in a community that voiced its displeasure fervently, a community whose first wave of refugees decades earlier were the political and economic ethnic elites. It was they who set the tone for what we considered legitimate ex-pressions of cultural identity. We learned in a national context that saw refugee flight as a way of recuperating American identity after a devastating military defeat in Vietnam.[5] But the United States is not the only country where we see contestations about what it means to be Vietnamese; we also find examples in France, Canada, and Australia in ways related to how each country received refugees.

But what about countries where Vietnamese border crossers were not primarily refugees? This question corresponded serendipitously with my continuing interest in Germany. I had been practicing German with online tools through the Deutsche Welle, a public broadcast-ing company, when I stumbled across a piece by Sebastian Schubert aptly titled "Berlin's Vietnamese Wall." "The German capital is home to thousands of Vietnamese," the subheading read. "But the commu-nities in the East and those in the West remain divided, even 15 years after the fall of the Berlin Wall."[6] Sure enough, everyday Vietnamese people echoed this refrain when I began to conduct fieldwork in Berlin in summer 2013. On hearing about my interest in studying Vietnam-ese people in Germany, nonprofit workers, grocery store cashiers, res-taurant servers, and Buddhist lay worshippers alike emphasized that unlike elsewhere in the diaspora, Berlin and Germany had not one but two Vietnamese communities—and they did not get along.

The following pages unpack this pervasive sentiment that Vietnamese border crossers in Germany remain divided along Cold War lines. Lan, a woman from southern Vietnam who migrated to West Germany through family reunification for refugees, captured this attitude: "I look at Germans and I feel that they're so lucky. Why were they able to heal like that [after reunification] when we haven't?" (*Chị nhìn người Đức rồi chị cảm thấy họ may mắn quá. Tại sao họ có thể chữa lành như vậy khi mình chưa làm được?*)

Yet Germany's Cold War history structured lingering perceptions not only of the Vietnamese border crossers who lived on both sides of the Iron Curtain, but of native Germans as well. In fact, Germans still stereotype what they see as intractable differences between east and west. For people socialized in pre-reunification Germany, "more than 40 years of dual state structures has indeed contributed to the construction of two different nations,"[7] diverging in social, economic, and political histories. By contrast, Lan assumes that nations should converge when states do—that political reunification should likewise have socially reunified people who share an ethnonational identity. This logic has echoes in journalism and scholarship that continue to report on and wonder about persisting divisions among Germans.[8]

On the one hand, this expectation that Cold War compatriots should have reunified when their divided countries did reveals the enduring power of ethnonational thinking. Even if we know that traditions are invented and national myths constructed,[9] scholars recognize that people often experience the ethnic nation as an indisputable core of their identities. This book therefore takes seriously how everyday migrants, thousands of miles from the place many still call home, make sense of their social, cultural, and religious lives as ethnic Vietnamese.

On the other hand, enduring conflicts between former North and South Vietnamese, East and West Germans illuminate how border crossings can quickly alter ethnic nationhood and nationalism. These Cold War compatriots understand themselves to be nations divided by states, but the undoing of physical borders did not similarly undo social ones. Thus, this book at once acknowledges how fervently people experience ethnic nationhood while also speaking broadly to how border crossings disrupt and transform existing social identities and relations. The following pages unpack this central insight that border crossings transform ethnic nationhood and nationalism in consequential, enduring ways.

THE BORDER WITHIN

1

Border Crossings

BEFORE TÀI LEARNED HOW TO CRAWL, he had already crossed and been crossed by international borders.* Tài was born in northern Vietnam in 1954,† shortly before Việt Minh revolutionary forces defeated the French at the Battle of Dien Bien Phu. Throughout the summer, several countries met in Geneva to coordinate French withdrawal from present-day Vietnam, Laos, and Cambodia and resolve lingering matters related to the First Indochina War. The Geneva Agreements were the reason for the first border crossing of Tài's life, designating a provisional military line at the 17th parallel. This border swiftly came to signify two competing Cold War states: the Democratic Republic of Vietnam (DRV, or North Vietnam) and the Republic of Vietnam (RVN, or South Vietnam).[1] (See Map 1.1.)

As the borders of the state to which they belonged changed, Tài's parents seized on an opening provided by the Geneva Agreements to

---

* With the exception of Linh Thứu Pagoda, I have replaced the names of people and organizations with pseudonyms.

† I use capital letters when referring to the states and citizens of North and South Vietnam between 1954/55 and 1975, as well as when referring to nationalism oriented around the fallen Republic of Vietnam. I use lowercase when discussing people, places, and things outside that period.

Map 1.1 Map of Divided Vietnam. Source: Frieda Luna Schlör. Original shapefile from ArcGIS.

traverse that border. The accords provided for a three-hundred-day period of free movement during which "any civilians residing in a district controlled by one party who wish to go and live in the zone assigned to the other party shall be permitted and helped to do so."[2] Tài, his parents, and siblings would form part of an exodus of hundreds of thousands of Catholics who headed southward. After having been border-crossed by state formation, Tài and his family in turn crossed a border that would become international.

The war between the two Vietnams again gripped Tài in 1975, producing the third border crossing of his life. On April 30, Northern forces breached the presidential palace in Saigon, capital of South Vietnam. President Dương Văn Minh surrendered unconditionally. The victors reunified the two countries under the one-party Socialist Republic of Vietnam (SRV) and renamed the city of Saigon in honor of North Vietnamese leader Hồ Chí Minh.

Mirroring the border crossings they experienced in 1954, Tài's family responded to the reunification of Vietnam by attempting perilous escapes at sea. The first of Tài's siblings to flee Vietnam by boat was rescued by the West German ship *Cap Anamur* in 1980. Two years later, more of his siblings escaped as "boat refugees." In 1985, at age thirty-one, Tài sought his own escape. He drifted on the sea for a month before transitioning to a camp in Thailand, where he waited three years to be resettled.

Tài eventually relocated to a country that, like his homeland, had been border-crossed by the Cold War. In autumn 1989, he arrived in West Berlin, an exclave belonging to democratic West Germany but completely encircled by socialist East Germany.[‡] (See Map 1.2.)

As did other "contingent refugees" (*Kontingentflüchtlinge*), Tài received generous social assistance from his host country. He enrolled in language classes for nine months and soon secured a job with a company that, when we met in 2016, he had been working in for

---

[‡] I use capital letters when referring to the states and citizens of East and West Germany between 1949 and 1990/91. I use lowercase when discussing people, places, and things outside that period.

Map 1.2 Map of Divided Berlin. Source: Frieda Luna Schlör. Original shape-file from ESRI/ArcGIS's Geoportal Berlin/Verlauf der Berliner Mauer, 1989 and Geoportal Berlin/Ortsteile von Berlin.

nearly thirty years. Grateful for having been granted a new lease on life, Tài "see[s] [Germany] as [his] second homeland now" (*Chú coi đây là quê hương thứ hai rồi*).

Like Tài, Trinh also repeatedly crossed and was crossed by international borders. Born in North Vietnam in 1969, she grew up in a destitute postwar environment. She would not flee her homeland as Tài's family had, but she also did not inherit the social and economic benefits that flowed to the children of Communist Party officials. The offspring of households that "had merit with the revolution" (*có công với cách mạng*) received opportunities to go abroad beginning in 1980, when Vietnam formalized bilateral agreements with socialist states such as the Soviet Union and Bulgaria. To mitigate labor shortages in Eastern Bloc industries such as construction and textiles, Vietnam would soon send abroad contract workers from nonelite backgrounds as well. Trinh knew that having one family member working abroad would elevate the financial situation of the entire household. She therefore left home in 1989 at age twenty to begin factory work in Czechoslovakia.

Tài and Trinh arrived in their respective host countries just in time to be swept up in another momentous instance of state formation augured by the fall of the Berlin Wall. For nearly thirty years, the wall encircled West Berlin, preventing Easterners from escaping into the West. As political objects, borders "do not have a life independent of the political life of the countries of which they are the outer bark."[3] Hence, the collapse of the Eastern Bloc would call into question the configuration of existing borders.

Facing uncertainty about their dissolving host states, contract workers in the Eastern Bloc responded by repatriating to Vietnam, trying to convert their statuses from temporary worker to immigrant, or crossing borders in flux to resettle elsewhere in Western Europe. Trinh chose the third path, paying a guide to help her clandestinely enter reunified Germany in 1991. She filed for asylum in Frankfurt, where she took integration classes while awaiting the decision on her case. Her asylum claim rejected, Trinh would later legalize through right-to-stay legislation (*Bleiberecht*). By the time I met her in 2016, she had long gained fluency in German, established a business in eastern Berlin, and had conferred German citizenship on her children.

This book is about how Tài, Trinh, and other Vietnamese migrants in Berlin navigate the twin phenomena of state formation and international migration—together, border crossings. These border crossings powerfully shape Vietnamese migrants' social identities and their relationships with one another. The protagonists of this book arrived in West, East, or reunified Germany under an array of legal labels: contingent refugee, contract worker, international student, tourist, undocumented migrant. I consider all of these, including refugees, as types of migrants.[4] But as we will explore in the next two chapters, migrant labels fail to capture the diverse motivations and opportunities with which people cross international borders. Some people directly experience state violence but ultimately leave as contract workers; others do not face persecution but arrive abroad as refugees. More important, this "migrant/refugee binary" inundates us with assumptions about who deserves help and who does not, whose lives are worth protecting and whose are not.[5]

Although *The Border Within* at times invokes a migrant/refugee binary, it ultimately seeks to move beyond the binary. It recognizes that the specific labels under which people cross borders matter deeply for their life opportunities. Yet it also argues that there is much to be gained by reading the narratives of a diverse spectrum of migrants alongside one another. Doing so allows us to see, as political scientist Rebecca Hamlin so aptly captures, "that borders do violent work."[6] I therefore refer broadly to people who migrated under different labels and wove in and out of various such labels throughout their lives as border crossers.

For similar reasons, I refer to state formation as borders crossing over people.[7] "The border crossed us" is a rallying cry of the immigrants' rights movement in the United States. When we picture an invisible yet formidable boundary crossing over people, we glean how borders are not just "physical but also figurative or ideological" tools for defining belonging.[8] Examining the border-crossed, this book roots itself in the lived experience of people "who unquestioningly pursued the logic of autonomy in their daily lives."[9] They did not seek resistance or social transformation at every turn, but their thoughts and actions at times nonetheless produced transformative outcomes.

This book, then, is an exercise in analytically informed storytelling.[10] It is one that values "less theory, more description."[11] The book privileges this mode of knowledge production in the spirit of offering grounded, accessible insights that I hope will resonate far beyond the academy. The stories of this book's protagonists reveal how mightily they identify with their ethnic nationhood, even as they collectively dismantle the political project of ethnic nationalism—a different phenomenon.

By *nationhood*, I mean people's subjective sense of belonging. Nationhood relies "not just [on] internal claims to social solidarity, common descent . . . [but also] distinctiveness vis-a-vis other nations."[12] We can consider the classic example of Germans as sharing an ethnic nationhood. The Vietnamese protagonists of this book fervently believed in and acted on shared ethnic nationhood, their feelings of belonging to a community of members who presumably share something in common with one another that they do not share with those outside the national club.[13]

By contrast, *nationalism* is the political principle that each nation should have its own state because "the political and the national unit should be congruent."[14] Actors work toward this goal through "project[s] to make the political unit, the state (or polity) congruent with the cultural unit, the nation."[15] Extending our example of German nationhood, we would expect nationalist politics to demand that Germans have a state for Germans and that members of the nation should not be divided by state borders. But as the following chapters delve into, the Vietnamese subjects I spent time with in Berlin by and large have abandoned this ethnonationalist project.

More broadly, this book argues that border crossings transform ethnic nationhood and nationalism in ways we miss when we look at state formation or international migration separately. Numerous historical examples reveal how border crossings *create* new nationhoods. Colonial borders crossed over people throughout the world, spurring the categories of Indian, Kenyan, and so forth.[16] People crossing over borders also produced new national categories, as with the emergence of Korean nationhood alongside large population movements within the expanding Japanese Empire.[17] In this book, Vietnamese-speaking people identified with the northern, central, or southern regions where they had lived since before French colonization. But the creation of the states of North and South Vietnam in the mid-twentieth century would crystallize these regional identities into national ones, aligned with competing states. People would lug these national identities with them to Germany, where outside observers readily detect that "North and South Vietnamese were and still are today strangers to each other."[18]

Border crossings also allow people and communities to *reproduce* ethnic nationhood and nationalism in particular ways. This happens when people stay put but borders change, as with the unexpected yet extensive ethnopolitics linked to the dissolution of the Soviet Union, Czechoslovakia, and Yugoslavia.[19] It also happens when people cross borders and, in doing so, reformulate their understandings of the nation abroad. In this way, 13 million emigrants who went abroad converted their local allegiances to a national Italian one.[20] Although cultivated in the Vietnamese homeland, Southern nationalism would live on through the dispersal of southerners after reunification. Northerners would transport abroad their belief that with Vietnamese reunification long settled, people from different regions were "one family" represented by the Socialist Republic of Vietnam. Yet they would come to find this ethnic nationalism highly contested.

By thinking about border crossings jointly, we see how they can powerfully *transform* nationalism in surprising ways. Contract workers, refugees, and later migrants alike would come to abandon the ethnonationalist project, no longer believing that their shared ethnic nationhood demands a shared state to which they all belong. This loosely echoes scenes from the US Capitol insurrection on January 6, 2021, when White nationalists brandishing the Confederate flag were joined by Vietnamese Americans with the yellow flag of fallen South Vietnam. Both flag wavers shared "a radicalized nostalgia for a lost country and a lost cause."[21] The subjects of this book have similarly transnationalized their ethnic nationalism. I do not mean this simply in the sense that their actions and allegiances span state borders. Rather, refugees have merged their devotion to South Vietnam with a commitment to the German nation-state. This latter commitment is key: it is not that they are waiting with bated breath for the fall of communism in Vietnam. Contract workers have also come to see refugees as falling outside the nation-state, even as they all presumably belong to a shared nation. This book is therefore centrally concerned with how Vietnamese people in Berlin rebuilt their lives after war and numerous disruptive border crossings. It highlights how they go about their routines thinking about or ignoring, interacting with, or shunning coethnics.

The Border Within thus explores how border crossings create, reproduce, and, crucially, transform ethnic nationhood and nationalism on the ground. It traces the creation of North and South Vietnamese nationhood and nationalism in the mid-twentieth century and analyzes how people deploy their nationalist allegiances in Germany today. The book unearths how everyday Vietnamese people's sense of ethnic nationhood has persisted even as their understandings of and commitments to ethnic nationalism have changed. Border crossings do not always produce these outcomes of persistent ethnic nationhood and transformed ethnic nationalism. But this was so with the Vietnamese people in Berlin whose stories underpin this book. More broadly, the book maintains that thinking about state formation and international migration as mirrored processes of border crossings can lend insight into how and why ethnic nationhood and nationalism might change in contradictory ways.

Nationals and Nationalists

The division of Vietnam in 1954 forged competing states that both adhered to the conviction that state and nation should coincide.

Contract workers and refugees, Northerners and Southerners alike grew up in rival Vietnamese states that each emphasized "the unity of the Vietnamese people and of their history and culture," the "governments both in Hanoi and in Saigon claim[ing] to speak on behalf of all Vietnamese."[22] Accordingly, Tài and Trinh referred to other Vietnamese, regardless of their regional identities or citizenship, as brothers and sisters (*anh chị em*) or as compatriots (*đồng hương*). Everyday people translated this rhetoric into action as well: after the fall of the Berlin Wall, refugees like Tài called in sick to work or skipped university classes to trudge the wintry streets of Berlin in search of contract worker coethnics. Once they located contract workers, refugees provided them with shelter, food, and assistance with filing paperwork to stay in Germany. Trinh also recalled the refugees who came to visit her and other contract workers in the asylum camps.

But even as Vietnamese people carried their sense of shared ethnic nationhood across borders, the state formations they lived through left indelible marks on their identities, sowing the seeds for enduring tensions. Everyday people would map regional and migration labels onto Cold War politics, assuming that refugees were South Vietnamese who, because of their anticommunism, fled and resettled in West Germany. Contract workers are correspondingly assumed to be North Vietnamese who, because of their communism, received the opportunity to go to the Eastern Bloc. Where the division of Vietnam created the categories of North and South, the movement of individuals across international borders further produced a migrant/refugee binary.

Trinh noted, for example, that even refugees who visited the asylum camps showed prejudice toward contract workers. They did so subtly when they commented on her northern accent or made off-handed remarks about communism. Trinh suspected that southerners—meaning, refugees—despised northerners because of the loss of South Vietnam.

Conversely, refugee Tài recalled his frustration after housing more than half a dozen contract workers in the early 1990s. Tài came home from work one day to find his apartment nearly set on fire because his guests had thrown a lit cigarette butt into the trash can. In the years following German reunification, former contract workers made headlines for illicit cigarette sales and gang violence.[23] From his personal encounters and developments in the former East, Tài concluded that "wheresoever communists arrive, wheresoever communists dominate, there is deceit there" (*hễ mà nơi nào cộng sản tới, hễ mà nơi nào mà cộng sản thống trị, thì nơi đó có sự gian dối*).

Tài was indeed a self-identified anticommunist southerner who received refugee status in West Germany, and Trinh a northerner who went to the Eastern Bloc for labor, but when we inspect their narratives more closely, we can already see that the dichotomies of North/South, migrant/refugee, communist/anticommunist were porous. Although he resolutely identifies with the fallen Southern regime, Tài was born in the north and speaks with a discernable northern accent. And despite being sent abroad by the communist Vietnamese state, Trinh would later participate in anticommunist protests to bolster her asylum claims in reunified Germany. Rather than "a simplistic division between communist and anti-communist identities," we begin to see "the duplicity and multiple identities that communist societies often produced."[24] And because Vietnam signed labor agreements with Eastern Bloc states after 1975, contract workers came from throughout the reunified country rather than just the north.

Even as they frequently reproduced Cold War binaries, the Vietnamese subjects of this book also recognized the murkiness of these categories. They knew that Northerners had also been persecuted by the Northern government, that people from the former North fled violence but were less likely to be recognized by Western countries as refugees,[25] and that southerners went abroad as contract workers after 1980. But even as they lament ongoing coethnic tensions and problematize these binaries, everyday Vietnamese people still reproduced them in their speech and actions. This book therefore examines how Vietnamese border crossers in Berlin "engage and enact (and ignore and deflect) nationhood and nationalism in the varied contexts of their everyday lives."[26] It examines how they talk, choose, perform, and consume the nation in their homes, at their workplaces, and during cultural or religious festivities. Day to day, nationhood rarely frames how people make decisions and interpret their actions. But as the following chapters reveal, the nation was intensely salient for Vietnamese people in Berlin.

Why, then, do these homeland divisions persist long after the geopolitical events that created them have changed? Drawing on themes that everyday people evoked organically, *The Border Within* takes as its starting point the conviction of Vietnamese border crossers that they belong to an unquestionably shared ethnonational fabric, one that unites northerner and southerner, contract worker and refugee, communist and anticommunist under the same banner of ethnic nationhood. Vietnamese enact these understandings of shared nationhood, such as when Tài welcomed northern contract workers into his home. The book then investigates when and how conflicts permeate coethnic relationships or prevent people from having them altogether. It contends that border crossings have preserved everyday Vietnamese people's sense of nationhood while working to undo their commitment to ethnic nationalism.

In their words and actions, Vietnamese border crossers embody divergent attitudes toward ethnic nationalism. Trinh's approach pivots on commonplace practices involving the red flag with a yellow star and other forms of "banal nationalism."[27] Her practice of nationhood is not state centered, but it does take for granted the legitimacy of a Vietnamese nation-state. By contrast, Tài has welded together his devotion to former South Vietnam and present-day Germany. As we will see, there is little room for northerners in Tài's nationalist commitments. His politics expose the unmaking of ethnic nationalism. Tài may speak of and act on an imagined bond with his ethnonational kin, but he sees no contradiction in a political boundary cutting across an ethnic one. Vietnamese border crossers in Berlin demonstrate that while ethnic nationhood may be slow to change,[28] ethnic nationalism need not be.

The Border Within

Border crossings reorganize social identities in enduring ways, so that even individuals born after the Cold War encounter Berlin's "Vietnamese wall" today.[29] Born in central Vietnam in 1996, Kim came to learn about north and south divisions after coming to Germany as an international student in 2015. Kim and I first met at a Buddhist pagoda in western Berlin three months after she had arrived. Nineteen years old, she was navigating life abroad and alone for the first time. As border crossers in other times and places have done, Kim relied on coethnic networks to find housing, employment, and resources for navigating her studies. She rented a room with an older south Vietnamese woman who introduced her to the pagoda where we met. Kim also came to know northerners, including Trinh, through attending events hosted by a cultural organization, Friendship and Adventure. And she would come to learn from them about the border within.

This book trains its gaze on how Vietnamese in Berlin erect boundaries against people they see as their coethnics, highlighting how distinctions within a group shape their social identities and dynamics with one another. As she grew up in Vietnam, for example, Kim used words such as *northerner* and *southerner* to describe a regional identity rather than a political one. She did not even know the word for the reeducation camps (*học tập cải tạo*) in which suspected Southern loyalists toiled. But during her first year abroad, Kim came to learn about the war from her housemate and others at pagoda. Attending events in west and east Berlin, Kim came to understand that her elders viewed Vietnamese reunification through starkly different lenses as either liberation or defeat. The labels of "north" and "south" became, for Kim, politicized. She herself would become labeled a southerner in both northern and southern spaces. Competing nationalisms thus come to encompass individuals born long after the war in Vietnam, who become sorted into Cold War divisions after leaving the homeland.

Much of what we know about the consequences of border cross-ings comes from the study of conflict among different ethnicities or nationalities. Ethnic conflicts after the fall of the Soviet Union, for example, revealed how state formation raises questions of belonging. Out of the ethnic cleansing in Yugoslavia emerged Croatia, Slovenia, Macedonia, Bosnia and Herzegovina, and Serbia and Montenegro. But even in these seemingly straightforward cases, state formations did not proceed so neatly according to the one-nation, one-state principle.[30]

Classic migration scholarship has also highlighted relations among groups, sketching how foreigners integrate into a main-stream.[31] But scholars increasingly draw attention to the fact that all immigrants are emigrants,[32] whose identities and practices are also informed by coethnics elsewhere in the diaspora.[33] Border crossers' identities are shaped not only in relation to homelands;[34] they are also shaped in relation to "elsewhere" places that are neither home-land nor host country.[35] These diverse frameworks reveal how global migration structures everyday relationships not just between mi-grants and their host society, but with the people left behind, as well as with coethnics abroad.[36]

This book focuses on such relationships among coethnics abroad, specifically in Berlin. The Vietnamese subjects presented in these pages behaved in many ways just like border crossers in different places and times, seeking out coethnics for emotional and material support. They rely on reports from friends and families abroad when considering their departures from a homeland, as Tài did.[37] Often they rely on coethnics to help them navigate illicit border crossings, as Trinh did.[38] Newly arrived in a host country, border crossers look for in-language assistance from coethnics, as Trinh did in the early 1990s and as Kim would in 2015.[39] As they settle, border crossers draw on ethnic social capital to navigate their children's schooling and trans-mit their cultural practices to the next generation.[40] Yet coethnic net-works are also fraught with conflict and exploitation.[41]

Examining people who share an ethnonational identity, we can trace how differences within a group play a role in constructing ethnic nationhood and nationalism.[42] Border crossers may experience the pull of shared ethnicity powerfully, believing that their "ethnic membership was acquired through birth and thus represent[s] a 'given' characteristic."[43] But shared ethnicity does not necessarily lead to a closely knit community.[44] Coethnic tensions cut across religious, national, cultural, and political lines. Indian Americans who practice Islam, for example, may feel more affinity toward Pakistani Americans who share their religion than toward Hindu Indian Americans who share their ethnonational background.[45] Relationships among coethnic migrants thus reveal how a "border is something immigrants bring with them."[46]

Border crossers do not simply reproduce their homeland divisions intact; rather, they alter them in the process. Yet this is difficult to disentangle when border crossers often leave their homelands at different times. Coethnics who migrate years or decades apart differ in more than just age or generation; they leave a homeland at a particular moment and out of a social milieu that continues to evolve. They also enter host countries with shifting policies and attitudes toward foreigners. This difference in time both reflects and shapes migrants' life opportunities and patterns of socialization. First-wave Cubans to the United States, for instance, encountered a context that courted their high human capital and treated their flight as a rejection of the Cuban Revolution. Decades later, neither the general US public nor émigrés looked favorably on expellees from the Cuban port of Mariel.[47] Instead, both saw Marielitos as either criminals or economic migrants guilty by association with communism.[48] Experiences with the homeland and varying degrees of belonging to the host country therefore inform the attitudes, experiences, and relationships of coethnics across immigrant cohorts.[49]

It is here that *The Border Within* makes a key intervention: it mines a comparison of dual migration streams from the same country of origin to what would later become the same country of destination. Comparing migration streams that began roughly simultaneously, this book holds constant the homeland context at the time people exited, as well as the time that they spent abroad. Vietnamese refugees resettled in West Germany in 1979/80, when contract workers also arrived in Eastern socialist states. Both types of border crossers encountered host states that saw them as exemplars of democracy or socialism and provided them with tools to navigate their lives abroad.[50] After German reunification, many contract workers would achieve the same level of language proficiency as refugees, and some would also naturalize into German citizenship. So although individuals' distinctive pathways to Germany shaped their trajectories, their migration routes did not predetermine their outcomes. By leveraging these concurrent migration streams, this book shows that coethnic divisions do not result strictly from disparities in integration into the host country.[51]

The Border Within excavates how border crossers import divisions from the homeland, all the while crafting identities and practices that challenge ethnic nationalism in the host country. The book investigates the changing meanings and practices of ethnic nationhood and nationalism across borders as international migrants weave their home and host societies together.[52] Migrants come from homelands that are internally fractured along ethnic, racial, religious, or other political lines. Such cleavages may at times be less apparent than in Vietnam, which formalized division in 1954. This book, then, illuminates social processes that are perhaps less obvious in instances where state formation has not (yet) occurred. Namely, that the mirrored processes of state formation and international migration restructure the relationships among people, state, and territory. These developments in turn transform ethnic nationhood and nationalism.

The Citizen-State-Territory Nexus

Tài and Trinh are not unique in traversing the borders of a home state that also redrew its lines; in fact, state formation and international migration often follow, or provoke, one another. States in the process of reconstituting may incite emigration, as we saw with flight from Cold War Cuba, Vietnam, and Poland. States in formation can also court immigration, as with the arrival of hundreds of thousands of

Jews to the Middle East after the creation of the state of Israel. Even when they have not recently experienced regime change, states may still influence migration. The People's Democratic Republic of Korea, for example, has long obstructed the exit of its citizenry. However, states in formation face an especially pressing need to control their populations as they consolidate power. States may thus impede or in- cite migration, to varying degrees of success.

International migration can also spark state formation. When peo- ple flee en masse, they delegitimize states. This was true, for example, of East Germans whose exit during the Cold War prompted domestic protest movements.[53] States respond forcefully to the threat of mass exit, as the example of the Democratic Republic of Vietnam reveals. After nearly 1 million Northerners migrated southward in 1954, the DRV took steps to prevent exit despite the Geneva Agreement's call for freedom of movement. Conversely, states can exploit ideas of the nation to justify expansionist policies. Weimar Germany did so in the early twentieth century, drawing on the image of persecuted Germans abroad to justify its eastward advance.[54] In both the long and the short terms, international migration can influence the machinations of states. Hence, state formation and international migration mutually reinforce one another.

State formation redefines who belongs as a member by changing either the state that governs or the territory in which a person lives, or both. This in turn calls into question the nationalist principle of one nation, one state. Nationalist movements spanning the globe demand state formation. These include Berbers in North Africa, Moros in the Philippines, Scots in the United Kingdom, Somalilanders in Somalia. Such movements seek to reorganize political space so that the state that governs over a territory will represent an imagined nation. State formation can also crosscut nations, creating new ones in the pro- cess. This happened with Tài and Trinh when mid-twentieth-century political changes recast Vietnamese people as belonging to either the North or the South.

International migration also challenges the idea that a state alone governs over a specified territory and that its sovereignty ends at its borders. As a process, international migration takes the national or citizen beyond the territory of a home state and into the jurisdiction of another state. When citizens leave their home soil, they stretch the reach of their homeland's sovereignty: tourists, international students, and migrants residing abroad have embassies and consulates that represent members of their countries of citizenship. This was true for Trinh, who regularly encountered the Vietnamese state during her labor stint in Czechoslovakia. This legal reach reveals how international migration is a process of "pull[ing] one society onto the territory of another state . . . linking 'here' and 'there.'"[55] Migrants further link *here* and *there* through their social, economic, and political activities in the host country oriented toward the homeland or directly in the homeland.

Yet refugees are thought to be distinct in that they sever the links among citizen, state, and territory.[56] By clandestinely departing a country, refugees often forfeit their citizenship. When this happens, they fall outside the nation-state-territory nexus because they lose the only membership that matters for the protection of rights.[57] Refugees are therefore assumed to rupture the citizen-state-territory trinity in a way that national minorities or nonrefugee migrants do not.

In contrast, this book maintains that border crossings more generally restructure the relationship among citizen, state, and territory. State formation allows people such as Cold War Germans, Koreans, and Vietnamese to acclimate to the reality of one imagined nation spread across several states. International migration allows people to carry their ideas of the nation and, at times, their national memberships with them abroad. This further challenges the bounds of territory in the citizen-state-territory trinity. Stretching any part of this nexus of people, state, and place correspondingly tests the principle of national and political congruence.

Border crossings transform national membership and nationalist convictions, and they do so jointly in ways that can produce incongruent nationalisms even among people who feel unhesitatingly that they belong to a shared nation. Border crossers from a variety of backgrounds demonstrate this when they carry with them certain cultural practices from a moment frozen in time, though things have long since changed in the homeland. Vietnamese diasporans, for example, widely consumed nostalgic pre-1975 music after leaving Vietnam. Meanwhile, the SRV government sought to block it in the homeland, deeming it anticommunist.[58]

The following pages illustrate the long-term consequences of these interconnected processes of border crossings. When state formation and international migration involve crossing external borders, people who cross these borders also erect internal ones. This book traces the development of these divisions in the homeland of Vietnam and examines how they have manifested in the host country of Germany.

Methodology

By conducting ethnographic fieldwork and interviews, I situated individuals' nationalisms in the "social organisational contexts (e.g. families, workplaces . . .) which mediate more structural (macro) dimensions of the nation."[59] Whether in public or private settings, Vietnamese border crossers thematized their regional and migration identities immediately and without prompting. This was true even in religious spaces that emphasized unity. I encountered this open contradiction in July 2014 when I first arrived at Chùa Linh Thứu, a Buddhist pagoda in western Berlin.

Within minutes, I realized the separation between northerners and southerners in this religious space. Two northern Vietnamese lay worshippers who were tidying up in the kitchen greeted me, sat me down, and offered me a hot bowl of vegetarian noodles before sending me down to the basement kitchen. There, half a dozen southern disciples were helping the nuns prepare food. All the while, the southern disciples sang "Saigon Is Beautiful," and bantered with one another about whether girls from Saigon or My Tho, in the Mekong Delta, were more beautiful. That day, the abbess granted me permission to conduct research at the pagoda.

The weeks raced by as I ran errands for the nuns and interviewed disciples who had been with the pagoda since its inception. Like many other people I would come to know over the next two years, the pagoda members gave generously of their time and stories. One of the nuns insisted I stay in the guest quarters instead of taking public transportation two hours each day to and from the pagoda. One of the disciples, a southern woman in her fifties, took pity on this young graduate student thousands of miles from home. She invited me over for the weekend at her apartment, where we talked well into the morning about religion, politics, and Vietnam. Not all of the relationships I formed would prove to be so intimate, but they always invited an opportunity to witness how people narrated their lives, how they navigated interactions with coethnics and natives, and how they talked about shared nationhood versus how they erected boundaries with coethnics. When I returned to Berlin in 2015, one of the disciples I met the year before pointed me to pagodas in eastern Berlin that were attended nearly entirely by northerners and former contract workers.

Through disciples at the pagodas, I came to participate in the two cultural organizations where I met Tài and Trinh: Refugees for Germany (RfG) and Friendship and Adventure (FaA). As I explore in a later chapter, the organizations had not only starkly contrasting memberships but also different practices of the nation. They also dealt with newcomers differently. Tài did not speak to me the first day I visited RfG. Instead, the uncle who invited me to their gathering ushered me into the kitchen to talk with the aunts. Only two weeks later did I finally speak to Tài. At that point, he started to inquire about my upbringing in the United States, revealing that he had already heard a bit about me. In a gesture of friendliness, he quipped that everyone in the United States speaks English (*tiếng Anh*). I replied delicately that this was not true, to which he implored me to listen carefully: women speak *tiếng anh*—a play on words about what women call their male partners (*anh*). I laughed, seemingly passing his screening test.

Trinh also did not say much the first time I met her earlier that same month, though not out of a need to determine my background. We met at an FaA holiday party, where she was busy eating and chatting with other members. One of FaA's leaders made an announcement introducing me and encouraging the aunts and uncles present to support my studies. Trinh's husband, Nghĩa, sat across from me at the table and, after a short greeting in which he heard my southern accent, remarked that "Saigon girls speak sweetly" (*con gái Sài Gòn nói chuyện ngọt ngào*). Trinh and I laughed, and the couple agreed that day to help me. On weekends over the next few months, I would chat with Tài at barbecues and parties and Trinh and Nghĩa at other barbecues and parties. I would occasionally attend events with Tài and also Trinh and Nghĩa outside RfG or FaA, such as Lunar New Year celebrations around the city. (See Table 1.1.)

Through the religious and cultural organizations that led me to Tài, Trinh, and many others, I interviewed eighty-one people who identified as Vietnamese.[60] Most of them were former contract workers, refugees, or their relatives who migrated through provisions for family reunification. To a lesser degree, I also spoke with international students, people who arrived on tourist visas but regularized through other channels, as well as a few second-generation Vietnamese Germans. The interviews lasted two hours on average. Most allowed me to record our interviews, which were nearly always in Vietnamese. Additionally, I shadowed several key respondents in their personal lives, sharing meals at their homes or mine, sitting with them during work shifts. (See Table 1.2.)

As the following chapters unfold, I discuss how my background as a Vietnamese American and the daughter of a former Southern army officer shaped my access to both northerners and southerners. I also compare my experiences with those of a female researcher born and raised in northern Vietnam, reflecting on our challenges, how we navigated suspicion, and the varying degrees to which we built trust.

Road Map

This book unfolds across six chapters that probe the long-term consequences of border crossings for ethnic nationhood and nationalism. Together, Chapters 2 and 3 present the book's first narrative arc, uncovering the genesis of the identities created by border crossings. After the division of Vietnam, the governments of the North and the

Table 1.1 Sample Characteristics (*n* = 81). Source: Author.

	%	Range
Migration pathway		
Refugee	16	
Refugee family reunification	12	
Contract worker	22	
Contract worker family reunification	14	
International student	14	
Visa (overstayer)	8	
Undocumented	7	
Other	7	
Age		20–76
Generational status		
1st	76	
1.5	18	
2nd	6	
Sex		
Male	43	
Female	57	

NOTE: Migration pathways are listed by the initial labels under which people arrived in West Germany, East Germany, the Eastern Bloc, or reunified Germany. Over time, some individuals' statuses changed categories.

Table 1.2 Key Respondent Characteristics. Source: Author

	Sex	Birth Decade	Birth Region	Migration Path	Migration Decade
Anh	F	1950	South	Visa	1990
Chau	F	1960	South	Refugee family reunification	1980
Chính	M	1960	South	Refugee	1980
Hạnh	F	1980	North	International student	2010
Hải	M	1970	North	Undocumented	2010
Hòa	M	1950	South	Refugee	1980
Hồng	F	1950	South	Visa	1990
Huệ	F	1940	North	Contract worker	1980
Kiều	F	1950	North	International student	1970
Kim	F	1990	Central	International student	2010
Lan	F	1960	South	Refugee family reunification	1980
Liên	F	1980	North	Marriage migrant	2000
Nghĩa	M	1960	North	Contract worker	1980
Sơn	M	1940	North	Contract worker	1980
Tài	M	1950	North	Refugee	1980
Tín	M	1940	South	Refugee	1980
Trịnh	F	1960	North	Contract worker	1980
Xuân	F	1990	North	International student	2010

NOTE: Kiều and Tài were born in the north and speak with northern accents but identify as southerners. Kim was born in the central region but speaks with a southern accent and is read as southern. The remaining respondents identify with their regions of birth.

South engaged in nation-making processes that involved rewarding loyalty and punishing disloyalty. The Cold War Vietnamese states constructed internal enemies and heroes through policies and identification documents. State formation in 1954 recast Vietnamese northerners as Northerners and southerners as Southerners. State formation in 1975 hardened this identity for the latter group. Just as everyday people experienced the Cold War unevenly, so too would they experience its conclusion asymmetrically.[61]

Chapter 3 examines how border crossings crafted the labels of refugee and contract worker. It sketches the pathways of border crossers to Cold War Germany and the Eastern Bloc before a groundswell of state formations swept across Central and Eastern Europe. Just as the dissolution of North and South Vietnam did not erase the identities of Northerner and Southerner, the dissolution of East and West Germany did not erase the identities of contract worker and refugee. In post–Cold War Berlin, regional identities and migration labels have fused together, with "southerner" being shorthand for "refugee" and "anticommunist," and "northerner" for "contract worker" and "communist." The reality, however, looks much messier. Chapters 2 and 3 jointly reconstruct the identities produced by border crossings, identities that persist even after the conditions that created them changed.

Pulling the narrative to the present day, Chapter 4 offers a second arc, looking at how Vietnamese people think and talk about the nation after border crossings. It follows a northern couple, Liên and Hải, as they lead their arduous lives. They interpret their struggles as the burden of belonging to a corrupt nation-state. Border crossers such as Liên and Hải envision southerners and former refugees as falling outside the Vietnamese nation-state, even as they talk about southerners and refugees abroad as part of a shared nation. Nationhood is perhaps always hierarchical, but the hierarchy here relates counterintuitively to membership.[62] By belonging, northerners represent what some see as a failed state; by forfeiting belonging, southerners embody a developed and free German one.

The final arc of this book delves into how the identities created by border crossings shape coethnics' social interactions and relationships with one another. Chapter 5 examines how competing Vietnamese identities inform friendship networks. It follows two women as they straddle the north-south divide: Anh, a southern economic migrant in her sixties, and Hạnh, a northern international student in her thirties. The chapter traces their failed attempts to enter both northern and southern spaces. People who do not fit the combinations of southern refugee and northern contract worker nevertheless become funneled into these allegiances. One way that Berlin's Vietnamese Wall persists, this chapter shows, is through group enforcement of social divisions.

Chapter 6 focuses on how Vietnamese enact coethnic boundaries in a shared religious space that strives for harmony. In winter 2016, attendees fill Linh Thứu Pagoda in western Berlin to celebrate the Lunar New Year. During the feast after morning prayers, wistful diasporic songs play in the background, recalling the loss of South Vietnam. Hồng, a southern migrant, turns to me midway through a song to point out that all of the music is from the south—implying to whom the pagoda belongs. This chapter illustrates how coethnics pull secular hostilities into a religious space that highly values accord. It reveals how different arenas of social life become absorbed into Cold War divisions.

Chapter 7 encapsulates the book's main thrust: border crossings shape ethnic nationhood and nationalism in inconsistent, quotidian, enduring ways. The creation of North and South Vietnam border-crossed individuals, converting their regional identities into political ones. Cold War migrations to Europe melded these identities of North and South with those of contract worker and refugee. By crossing an international border, ordinary Vietnamese people pull societies together, allowing Southern nationalism to live on even though the South has fallen, and even as people living in contemporary Vietnam go about their daily lives in recognition of this. Finally, the understandings and practices that people retain, discard, or adapt after border crossings structure the formation of communities for generations, enveloping even those who were born long after the war had ended.

The Border Within affirms the importance of nation-states in the lives of those who cross and are crossed by borders. Tài, Trinh, and many of their coethnics consider Vietnamese from different regions of origin and migration backgrounds to be one people, yet the company they keep reveals that the Cold War divide lives on. This book insists that to understand why this is so, we need to consider ethnic nationhood as related to, but not synonymous with, ethnic nationalism. People can self-identify as part of an ethnic nation, but that identification does not mean they believe coethnics need to belong to a shared ethnic nation-state. Our first task, then, must be to trace the roots of these categories of North and South back to the homeland and the moment of national division.

2 Making Northerners and Southerners

In the nineteenth and twentieth centuries, the differences between northerners and southerners were sufficiently palpable that the assertion of a unified "national identity" was purely ideological and not an objective description of real life.

—Olga Dror, *Making Two Vietnams*

Twentieth-century Vietnamese poets often quoted, with understandable pride, the fifteenth-century poet Nguyen Trai's boast that Vietnam had "at no time lacked heroes." The corollary was that Vietnam had at no time lacked enemies.

—Marilyn B. Young, *The Vietnam Wars, 1945–1990*

THE VIETNAM OF TODAY, bordering China to the north and Cambodia to the west, did not exist before the early nineteenth century. The name now given to the nation-state began to circulate only in the early twentieth century. Before that, speakers of various Vietnamese dialects belonged to and largely peacefully coexisted with the Sinitic Empire.[1] In modern nationalist narratives, however, Vietnamese identity coalesced around war and fending off foreign aggressors. As the tale goes, Vietnamese repeatedly repelled the invading Chinese, who dominated "Vietnam" from the first century BCE to the ninth century CE. Vietnam then endured decades of French colonialism (1880s to 1950s) and a brief Japanese occupation (early 1940s).

This mythology around nationalist identity ignores how people who spoke various Vietnamese dialects largely identified with their villages, towns, or regions; moreover, they often directed their hostilities against one another. One historian, for example, has described the regional antagonisms between north and south as a "national pastime."[2] The regional categories that persist today partially trace their roots to differentiated rule under French colonization.[3] But although these local identities predate the twentieth century, the Vietnamese *national* identity is of more recent vintage. In fact, some high-ranking officials in mid-twentieth-century Vietnam identified as French nationals loyal to the faraway "motherland."[4] By the mid-twentieth century, however, both Vietnamese states promoted the idea that the Vietnamese "people" belonged to one ethnic nation. This included those across the 17th parallel. Such ethnic nationhood relies on myths of solidarity, common descent, and distinctiveness compared to other nations (Chapter 1).

Twentieth-century geopolitics fashioned two Vietnamese states that were unified in their desire for independence from colonial powers but divided in their chosen governance systems. In 1954, forces led by the Việt Minh (League for the Independence of Vietnam) dealt the French a decisive military defeat at Dien Bien Phu. Having ousted the French, Hồ Chí Minh and the Việt Minh earned the admiration of large swaths of the population. The timing could not have been more opportune, taking place the day before the start of negotiations in Geneva to end the First Indochina War.[5]

The resulting Geneva Agreements stipulated nationwide elections in 1956 to create a single Vietnamese government. Yet the popularity of Hồ, Communist leader of the Democratic Republic of Vietnam (DRV), led onlookers to conclude that "Ho and the Viet Minh seemed certain to win" such an election.[6] The Geneva Agreements further provided for a cease-fire along the 17th parallel, splitting Vietnam in half.[7] Over the next year, however, Ngô Đình Diệm consolidated power in the South and solidified US backing, much to the chagrin of American officials working to undermine him. By 1955, Diệm proclaimed himself president of the Republic of Vietnam (RVN).[8]

As this chapter explores, the division of Vietnam would allow the DRV in the North and RVN in the South to craft two distinctive nations on either side of the 17th parallel. This boundary would come to represent opposing states and nations, albeit with a shared commitment to the nationalist principle of one nation, one state. Each side believed that it needed to liberate the other and reunify the country. Schools in the North, for example, impressed on children their duty to "liberate the South to unite the Fatherland."[9] Ngô Đình Diệm likewise exhorted citizens "to liberate the north and the millions of people suffering under the dominion of the red devils."[10]

For the next two decades, the North would wage political and military campaigns to reunify with the South under communism, and the South would seek to construct a Vietnamese national identity rooted in democracy, diversity, and anticommunism.[11] The North's political campaigns would ultimately prove more effective at framing the war for its citizenry. Phước's parents exemplify this. Attending school in North Vietnam, they learned nationalist myths about the bravery and moral superiority of their nation—a nation that fended off invading forces with far better training and weaponry. His parents' pride in their nation was bolstered by propaganda, as they later described it to their son. Indeed, the DRV instilled in young children "a sense of clear national direction and moral certainty in the conflict being waged in the RVN."[12] Convinced Communists, Phước's parents internalized state lessons about the suffering of Southerners under an American puppet.

Fighting in the People's Army of Vietnam, Phước's father believed unfailingly in the North's mission to liberate the South. Soldiers needed something to trust in and fight for, he explained to his son. On April 30, 1975, Phước's father was one of the soldiers who entered Saigon, capital of South Vietnam. Taking in the splendor of the city and the Saigonese who reacted with fear and resentment, Phước described his father as having an "oh shit" moment. Did a city that was so much grander than Hanoi need liberating? Had he been duped? But it was too late to reverse course. He was already part of the engine that would extinguish South Vietnam that day.

Sitting at a café in Berlin in 2016, Phước detailed his father's wartime experiences in a steady, occasionally ironic tone. His parents did not talk to him about the war when he was a child. As he neared adulthood in post-reunification Germany, Phước began to ask his parents about their lives during the war. Only then, decades later and thousands of miles away, did Phước's father convey how seizing Saigon had transformed him. Feeling culpable for his role in ensuring the spread of communism throughout Vietnam, Phước's father stopped believing in the revolution.

But for all that Phước had invoked communism in our conversations, it remained a nebulous, catch-all phrase. When I asked him to clarify what he meant by that word, he counted off the adjectives on his fingers: "That word [*communist*] . . . in my head, if I'm just free-associating: *Vietnamese, northerner*. You could say the generation before [reunification in] 1975." (*Cái từ đó . . . trong đầu anh, nếu mà anh chỉ assoziieren: Việt Nam nè, người bắc nè. Có thể nói là thế hệ trước năm 75.*) Phước speculated that no one truly followed communism anymore. But it endured as a label that he associated with himself, his parents, and people from his region of origin, despite their personal views. Hence, complex ideologies such as communism or anticommunism become labels that transcend what people actually believe. These labels come to define how people see themselves, even in the absence of matching political convictions.

Recounting his father's experiences, Phước illustrates how state- and nation-building processes go hand in hand: the creation of North and South Vietnam required both the development of structures of governance (state building) and the creation of citizens in a particular image (nation building). The competing Vietnamese states crafted their citizens in binary images of revolutionary communist or democratic anticommunist, even though some in the North did not believe in the revolution, and even as many in the South fought to overthrow the Saigon government.[13]

Although relatively rare in modern times, instances of state formation reveal how border crossings can swiftly create new nationhoods. By emphasizing the unity of the Vietnamese people across borders,

the North and South Vietnamese states espoused the nationalist principle that each nation should have its own state rather than being
spread across states. But by forging competing North versus South
Vietnamese governments, state formation led to separate Vietnamese
nationhoods.

States in formation produce new nationals by identifying who belongs versus who does not. As one of this chapter's opening quotes
conveys, modern Vietnamese figures staked pride in their nation's continued struggle against foreign enemies. In the Cold War context of the
twentieth century, these enemies came from within and without.

This chapter therefore foregrounds the making of internal enemies
and heroes in the North and South, focusing on how everyday people
experienced nation-building processes. We can think of the modern
state as "produced through a totalizing process. . . . [A] homogeniz-
ing thrust creates the nation as all those the state should administer,
because they supposedly have something in common."[14] To forge the
nation that a state should govern, North and South Vietnam needed
to propagate and enforce their distinct visions of a good citizen. Everyday people inferred these nation-building practices through state
actions to reward loyalty, such as through granting scholarships for
promising citizens to study abroad. States also penalized disloyalty
through imprisoning real or suspected dissidents. "To make the nation," then, "is to make people national."[15]

Crucially, both Vietnamese states created these internal distinctions between good and bad citizens. This is because state and nation
building often require the regulation of internal enemies, regardless of
whether the state is democratic or communist. To be sure, Ngô Đình
Diệm's First Republic in the South was notoriously undemocratic.
Nonetheless, we see the potential for all types of political regimes to
punish those it perceives to be enemies—for instance, through treason laws. As we shall return to in the following chapter, "the power
of states to purify the nation has caused and still causes the displacement of huge numbers of people."[16] We will also see this with the mass
departure of northern-born Vietnamese southward after the Geneva
Agreements.

Making Traitors and Heroes Out of Border Crossers, 1954

In 1954, the Cold War Vietnamese states began to transform regional identities into political categories of North and South by regulating population movement. Article 14(d) of the Geneva Agreements provided an early test of the Vietnamese states' reputations: it guaranteed people the freedom to move to the half of Vietnam where they wanted to live. The stipulation was originally intended for military regroupment, but hundreds of thousands of civilians would eventually resettle across the 17th parallel. The International Committee for Control, which oversaw these population exchanges, counted 892,876 people as having moved southward and 4,269 northward.[17] Yet other observers vary dramatically in their assessments of the number of people in these border crossings, one historian estimating that between 80,000 and 90,000 people moved northward with the aid of Soviet Bloc ships.[18] Despite divergent estimates, Western onlookers seized on the greater number of southward-bound migrants to claim that Vietnamese were "voting with their feet against communism."[19] Mass movement to the emerging South discredited the North during a critical Cold War juncture in which both governments vied for international recognition.

But people left the north for reasons other than strict opposition to communism. First, northerners faced food shortages in 1954 that reminded many of the famine that ravaged the region a decade earlier.[20] Famine and other "natural forces may, on closer scrutiny, reveal state negligence or indifference."[21] Indeed, the Japanese occupation and mismanagement of Vietnam in the early 1940s aggravated a famine that killed more than 1 million people.[22] The emergent South and its allies seized on this historical precedent to stoke fears of a return to starvation. They spread information about fertile, plentiful land awaiting northerners across the 17th parallel. Undercover agents also circulated rumors of impending American bombings and other calamities that would strike the north.[23] Using American, British, and French ships, the United States provided for the evacuation of northerners in Operation Passage to Freedom. In turn, a Polish boat, the *Jan Kilinski*, "transported nearly 85,000 people, and 3,500 tonnes of military equipment" from the south to the north.[24] For their part, northern authorities warned civilians of American treachery, murderous intent, and cannibalism.[25] Both sides thus fueled confusion around the division of Vietnam to facilitate or impede migration.

Second, the Catholic backgrounds of most of the northern migrants (*bắc di cư*) raised questions about religious persecution in the doctrinally atheist North. Catholics could draw on the historical record to justify their fears: in a 1930–1931 rebellion, communist agitators speared to death Father Pierre Khang, a Vietnamese priest.[26] When Vietnam divided two decades later, Catholic clergy in the North at times encouraged their parishes to move southward. "God is not here any more," they proclaimed.[27] Some lay Catholics feared being unable to attend church services once their leaders and coreligionists had all moved southward. In pamphlets, many referred to their migration as a forced displacement.[28] Yet more Catholics decided to stay than leave, making "concerns about religious freedom . . . themselves insufficient to explain the mass migration."[29]

Third, Ngô Đình Diệm, first president of the RVN, was a Catholic (albeit from the central rather than northern region). He exploited the momentum around southward migration to further his administration's political goals. For example, he resettled northerners to less populated areas in South Vietnam as a bulwark against rural populations that opposed his rule.[30] While Diệm's Catholic background alone did not convince his coreligionists to move southward, the then-Prime Minister and his American allies actively facilitated migration.

During fieldwork, I spoke with only one person whose family moved from the south northward in 1954 but met several who headed southward. Two such northern migrants, Tài and Kiều, offered some of the most searing criticisms of northerners and Communists. Both born in northern Vietnam right before the defeat of the French, Tài and Kiều were carried into the south as infants. Tài, whom we met in Chapter 1, pointed to his family's Catholicism as the reason they fled southward. Kiều, a devout Buddhist, frames this start to her life in bold terms: "I was already fleeing from Communists from the time I was one year old" (*Cô đã trốn cộng sản đi từ lúc cô một tuổi rồi*). Her

father fought with the French against Việt Minh forces at the Battle
of Dien Bien Phu, where he perished. Although the Geneva Agreements prohibited retaliation against individuals for their allegiances
during the First Indochina War, Kiều's mother believed they would
be denounced (đấu tố) as antirevolutionary. She carried Kiều into the
south just a month after her husband died. Kiều never met her father,
but the image of "[him] dying with the yellow flag" (bố cô chết với lá
cờ vàng) stayed with her throughout her life. She "never knew [recog-
nized] the red flag" (cô bao giờ biết cái cờ đỏ sao vàng là gì đâu).

Sixty years on and half a world away, northern border crossers like
Tài and Kiều demonstrate that the political identities of North and
South can eschew region of origin. They both identify as Southerners
and, when recounting their childhoods in the South, do not mention
hostilities around their northern origins. Historians have remarked
on the northern migrants' "resistan[ce] to assimilation" and southerners' distrust of the newcomers.[31] Catholic refugees from the north
also received government assistance, which exacerbated tensions between the new arrivals and local southerners.[32] But after 1975, people
originally from the north who speak with northern accents can con-
vincingly claim belonging to South Vietnam and suffering because of
its loss.

Tài's and Kiều's transformation into Southerners suggests that
nationhood can change rapidly after border crossings. This might
be surprising, considering that its political expression, nationalism,
"builds a link between cultural identity and geographical territory—
blood and soil."[33] Ethnicity, the basis of the nationalism undergirding
this book, can be slow to change.[34] And yet Tài's and Kiều's national
allegiances shirked their ties to northern soil. The Cold War division
of North and South Vietnam and the subsequent migration of northerners like Tài and Kiều challenged the tenet that "ethnic boundaries
should not cut across political ones."[35] Vietnamese like Tài and Kiều
had come to see themselves as one people but would diverge in their
competing national belonging to either the North or the South. In
practice, ethnic boundaries routinely cut across political boundaries
and vice versa. But rarely do they do so as markedly as when states

dissolve and reconstitute. The human tolls of state formation are tremendous, which is perhaps why the current configuration of states on the world map has changed remarkably little since the 1990s.[36]

Tài's and Kiều's national allegiances changed precisely because the "discourse of nationalism is inherently international."[37] Both Vietnamese governments sought recognition from other states that they alone, rather than their adversaries across the 17th parallel, were the legitimate arbiters of Vietnamese nationhood. Journalist Joshua Keating's metaphor of the world map as a club of countries captures this underlying logic. To be a member of the club, an aspiring country needs recognition by other members. The members may not always get along with one another, but together they serve as gatekeepers to entering the club. In the geopolitical context of the mid-1950s, two competing clubs operated, one led by the Soviet Union and the other by the United States. To achieve recognition in these clubs, the North and South Vietnamese states needed to set themselves apart from each other. To do so, they needed to deal with defectors or arrivals like Tài and Kiều. These new states also needed to monitor and reckon with those who remained. They often achieved this through documentation practices, legislation, and other forms of bureaucratic organization that shape the modern nation-state.[38]

Ma(r)king Good and Bad Northerners after 1954

Following the mass exodus of people southward in 1954–1955, the DRV instituted a household registration system for surveillance, population control, and state security. The household registration system in Vietnam (*hộ khẩu*) resembled China's (*hu kou*).[39] Household registries determined people's allocations for food and other vital supplies, as well as the right to move around the country. The registries provided official justification for the government to move families out of cities and into mountainous New Economic Zones (NEZ) to reduce urban density. The Ministry of the Interior "almost certainly" based the household registries on the "life history" (*lý lịch*),[40] "the logic and form [of which appears to] have their origins in the Soviet revolution, when the personal history form (*lichnyi listok*) appears to have been used in a party purge in 1921."⁴¹

The lý lịch inquired "into one's family, going back three or more generations, on the moral and political antecedents of all members."⁴² For example, a question on a 1990s version of the life history asks,

> BLOOD BROTHERS AND SISTERS (Also specify name, age, alias, birthplace, what they did for the enemy, for us. For each time period, state rank, position, branch. What are they doing now, where?) You need to specify for each time period from 1945–1954 and from 1955–April 1975. If you have many brothers and sisters, then write everything about one before moving to the next.⁴³

The form further interrogates social relationships outside the family and what role one's friends played in struggles against the French and, later, Americans.

In the mid-1950s, individuals could be grouped into different designations based on the household registries and, by extension, the life history:

> The letter [from Hanoi's Labor Department in 1956] grouped people into three categories: people available for work were identified as "mechanics", people not recommended for employment, and people identified as "problematic". The latter two categories included . . . children of landlords, someone with a "hesitating attitude", someone described as a "right arm of the clergy", an "anti-communist youth", a "hooligan", a man "whose father was living in France and who himself was often away from home without a reason", as well as someone holding a suspect [household registration].⁴⁴

The government wielded these life histories to mark and punish demonstrated antirevolutionaries. Importantly, it also used them to identify potential threats posed by people with "hesitating attitudes" or who seemed inappropriately indoctrinated into the communist state.

The life history created distinctions among citizens by marking some as heroes and others as "enemies of the people."⁴⁵ People identified as having a good background received government employment and related social advantages. A revolutionary background conferred advantages not only to oneself but also to one's children and grandchildren. This is exemplified by Ngọc Lan, who was born in North Vietnam in the early 1960s. Both her parents, committed socialists, served in the Vietnamese Workers' Party (later, the Communist Party of Vietnam). As we will see in Chapter 3, Ngọc Lan would later go abroad on a highly coveted labor contract precisely because of her parents' loyalty.

In the 1960s, both Vietnamese states also rewarded loyalty by providing international scholarships for students, which allowed them to escape war at home and train abroad. International students played key roles in state-building efforts. First, educational exchanges reflected and strengthened relationships between the allied countries that engaged in them. Second, one goal of such exchanges was to equip students with the tools for national reconstruction. North Vietnamese students in East Germany and the Soviet Union would largely specialize in technical disciplines, such as architecture and engineering, deemed critical for rebuilding after colonialism and war.[46]

Because he had the chance to go abroad while violence raged at home, Nam, from North Vietnam, felt obligated to study diligently: "We were able to go on the bones and blood of our friends who went to war. So the responsibility is to come here to eventually return to build the country. . . . We have to be responsible to the people who took up arms to fight." (*Bọn chú được đi là đi vào tiêu chuẩn xương máu của các bạn đi chiến đấu. Thì trách nhiệm của chú là sang đây học để cuối cùng là trở về để xây dựng đất nước. . . . Mình phải có trách nhiệm với những người cầm súng chiến đấu.*) As Nam neared completion of high school, the authorities had begun to deemphasize the life history. The Minister of Education determined that able students, even if they did not have spotless revolutionary backgrounds, were eligible to study abroad. Given his mediocre background, Nam considered himself especially fortunate to have received a scholarship. He thus experienced the Northern victory in 1975 as a reminder of how urgently he needed to return and pay his dues in Vietnam. Once he completed his studies, Nam repatriated and began a government internship for two years. In Chapter 3, we will return to how students like Nam would have a second opportunity to go abroad to lead labor contingents in the early 1980s.

Meanwhile, those with an antirevolutionary background faced "a denial of state employment, education, and host of other services necessary for survival in the socialist economy."[47] They passed these backgrounds onto their children and grandchildren. This group included the descendants of landowners who were punished during the reforms begun in the 1940s that came to fruition between 1954 and 1956.[48] As the Việt Minh solidified the DRV, it implemented a land reform to combat famine and redistribute wealth. Landowners should have been stripped of some of their land. In practice, they lost most, if not all, of their belongings. They also faced public denouncements, and many were executed. Historian Edwin Moise contends that between three thousand and fifteen thousand perished, historian Bernard B. Fall estimating fifty thousand, Richard Nixon putting the number at half a million.[49] Party leaders eventually acknowledged errors in how they implemented land reforms, but the program achieved its aims: "It eliminated anti-revolutionary class enemies in rural society, it instituted an ostensibly more equitable distribution of land usage, and it traumatized the rural population into obedience to the state."[50]

Born in the late 1940s in northern Vietnam, Sơn was one such person whose family inherited the status of antirevolutionary. "[His] maternal grandfather and paternal great-grandfather were denounced [as landowners] . . . denounced so then [his] maternal grandfather's side were shot." (*Ông ngoại với lại bố ông nội chú là bị đấu tố . . . đấu tố thì bên ông ngoại nhà chú là bị xử bắn.*) Thereafter, Sơn's parents had to swiftly redeem themselves:

> My parents then were obliged to follow the revolutionary path. To atone. . . . The other families for example had to put in a normal degree of effort. . . . My background was a child of a landowning household, so now you have to toil, so that they can see your labor. This is the way to reeducate.
>
> (*Bố mẹ chú lúc đấy là bắt buộc phải đi theo con đường cách mạng. Để chuộc tội. . . . Những gia đình khác thì thí dụ như là người ta chỉ làm với*

mức độ bình thường. . . . Thành phần của mình là con nhà địa chủ, thì
bây giờ mày đi làm là mày phải làm cật lực, làm sau để tao thấy được
cái công sức của mày. Cái đấy là cái để mà cải tạo.)

Their property confiscated, members of their family killed, and their
reputations tarnished, Sơn's parents had to labor for the party responsible for bringing about their family's downfall. His parents became
cadres, though "truthfully . . . if people participated [in the revolution]
like [his] parents but without the bad life history of [his] parents, then
they would have quickly advanced" (*Thật sự . . . nếu như những người*
mà hoạt động cách mạng như bố mẹ chú mà không phải cái lý lịch xấu
như bố mẹ chú thì sẽ rất là nhanh phong tiến). For his part, Sơn en-
listed in the army and fought in the war against South Vietnam. By the
end of the war in 1975, two generations of Sơn's family had sufficiently
proven themselves loyal to the revolution to merit a good background.
This change in Sơn's life history would translate into an opportunity
for him to work abroad in East Germany in the early 1980s.

In sum, the life history form allowed the nationalizing North Vietnamese state to categorize internal enemies as well as heroes. This is
because "identification documents are a key locus of this symbolic
power of the state" to create rather than simply describe categories of
people.[51] After all, the same people who would have been considered
enemies in the North became heroes when they arrived in the South.
The life history document therefore fashioned the very categories of
citizens it sought to designate—those the state could trust and reward
and those it distrusted and punished. Classifying and penalizing internal enemies are tried-and-true approaches of states' playbooks.
This applies beyond socialist states, the South Vietnamese state following the same playbook.

Ma(r)king Good and Bad Southerners after 1954

As in the North, the emerging South Vietnamese state differentiated
among the citizens it considered loyal versus treacherous. Only individuals whose entire families had remained neutral or fought with

the French against the Việt Minh could hold village administrative posts, for instance.[52] The Geneva Agreements formally barred retaliation against people on the basis of their allegiances during the First Indochina War. Nevertheless, the South Vietnamese government exercised "the right to determine 'who is a Resistance member and a patriot, who is a Vietcong saboteur.'"[53] The Ngô Đình Diệm regime "issued Ordinance Nos 6 and 47, which made support for Communism a capital offence."[54] Through Ordinances 48 and 53, it further "imposed forced assimilation on the Chinese community,"[55] presumably suspicious because of their communist ethnonational homeland.

Like the DRV, the RVN also rewarded individuals by sending them abroad to study. One example is Kiều, who was carried into the south as a baby in 1954. In the early 1970s, she received a scholarship to train as an engineer in West Germany. Her scholarship specified that she would return to South Vietnam after graduation. Although international students from both Vietnams shared a duty to repatriate after their studies, reunification would complicate this outcome for Southerners abroad. Like Kiều, many of them would become de facto refugees in their host countries.

As in the DRV, the RVN carefully selected certain figures, often fallen male soldiers, to be elevated as national heroes. Both states renamed streets after their respective national heroes, and both engaged in "Vichyite indoctrination practices by which government officials repeated to the[ir] peasants lectures" given by their respective leaders.[56] As in the DRV, the RVN sought to elevate some to martyrdom: in preparation for the National Day celebration in 1956, the RVN Department of Foreign Affairs had to exhume "fallen heroes who had fought against invaders . . . in order for their accomplishments to be cited with the nation."[57] Meanwhile, the Department of Education drafted biographies for these heroes. Various arms of the state apparatus therefore played a role in curating the image of national heroes.

Also mirroring campaigns in the North, Ngô Đình Diệm's RVN targeted suspected traitors. These took the form of denounce the communist campaigns (phong trào tố Cộng diệt Cộng),[58] which allowed the RVN to apprehend anyone it considered to be a security threat.

Beginning in late 1955, the government arrested tens of thousands who had fought with the Việt Minh against the French. Many were jailed or sent to reeducation camps.[59] To establish authority over the mountainous regions before communists could spread their influence there, Diệm settled hundreds of thousands of people to the Central Highlands. Finally, Diệm's government also drew on the RVN's military code to execute an RVN citizen for treason, making clear that the internal enemy "was being punished for his personal degeneracy as much as he was for his political dissidence . . . sen[ding] a broad warning about the grave consequences of attempting to subvert [Diệm's] government."[60] The regime was so consumed with identifying internal enemies that, for example, Diệm's civic action cadres in the countryside literally marked houses considered loyal with white or gold placards and homes of suspected Việt Cộng with black ones.[61]

Whether originally from the north or the south, the Vietnamese border crossers I spoke with often recalled the northern land reforms and DRV persecution of those considered antirevolutionary; not a single person, however, mentioned Diệm's "denounce the Communist campaign" or land reforms. No one recalled the southern individuals and groups who actively organized against the RVN government— despite Diệm heaping attention in his early rule toward "eliminating all political competition [in ways that] reminded southern nationalists of the Viet Minh in the first two years following the August Revolution [of 1945]."[62] One of Diệm's priorities on seizing power was to weed out internal, rather than external, enemies. Not one of my respondents recalled these struggles or Diệm's tenure having been dogged by "competition for ascendancy between the two groups that [eventually brought him down]: the Buddhist activists and the military officers."[63] Like US government officials, my respondents considered only those aligned with the government to be South Vietnamese—"though more often than not [RVN officials] were born in the North." The villages outside government control also "were [considered] Viet Cong and not South Vietnamese villages."[64]

Civilian Northerners understandably may have had limited and inaccurate information about the South, but why might this have also been the case for the Southerners living there? Analyzing the educational systems, organizations, and media in the DRV and RVN, historian Olga Dror provides a persuasive answer: the two states operated in vitally different ways in relation to the war. The DRV organized all facets of social life around the war, including "unleashing a barrage of opprobrium against the enemy," both the US and their Vietnamese allies. Children in the North learned that "there was a clear path: the war was against Americans, the North must expel them and take over the South, and build socialism there."[65]

Crucially, the RVN could not impose the same policies the DRV did because the South existed as an explicitly anticommunist Vietnamese state. It had to allow some measure of dissent, and the diverse religious, political, and social landscape of the South fueled this dissension. The RVN also sought to shield its children against the reality of war, so that "in the South, children did not know much about the North, or on what conditions the North and the South could be united." They largely succeeded, considering that many of the people Dror interviewed who had grown up in the South during that time did not know "who Ho Chi Minh was, what communism was about, and remained unsure about the reasons for the war."[66]

The actions of both Vietnamese states after 1954 offer a key lesson: nationalizing states deploy both carrot and stick in nation building. That they did so to varying degrees of effectiveness matters less than the fact that they both rewarded loyalty and punished disloyalty, whether real or perceived. The North and South both relied on bureaucratic practices toward these ends, and even the punishments they meted looked remarkably similar. Yet nearly half a century after the fall of South Vietnam, respondents from all regions failed to mention the power struggles that tarnished the South's reputation throughout its existence. They neglected the string of heavy-handed or weak-willed RVN leaders, as well as claims of political and religious persecution that inspired antiwar protests abroad. Even as they evoked the atrocities committed in the North by communists, respondents discounted similar occurrences in the South—that is, until after the communist victory.

Ma(r)king Enemies and Patriots in the South after 1975

Reunification in 1975 upended the lives not just of Vietnamese citizens living in the country but also of those studying abroad. Who these students were, what they did, and how they left their homelands did not determine their opportunities to resettle elsewhere. Instead, their migration channels diverged because of regime change that resulted in the formation of a new state.[67] The communist victory ensured that North Vietnamese international students would repatriate, if only temporarily. And it saw South Vietnamese international students transformed into refugees overnight.

South Vietnam collapsed before Kiều could complete her studies and repatriate. The RVN Embassy in Bonn closed, and Kiều's passport became obsolete. Kiều and other students in this situation had few options to return, given that reunified socialist Vietnam had strong motives to deny entry to Western-educated individuals. Such actions of the SRV created in the country of destination de facto refugees who had not left their homeland under conditions of fear or violence.[68] Kiều and most of her fellow international students stayed in West Germany, receiving refugee documents from the West German government.

In the reunified homeland, the three-generation life history that nearly curtailed Nam's chance to study abroad would soon come into play throughout the country. The SRV's documentation practices "ensure[d] that those whose families had supported [the RVN] were penalized."[69] As in both regions before 1975, households considered disloyal faced property confiscation, imprisonment in reeducation camps, and removal to largely uninhabited NEZs.[70]

Orphaned by the end of the war, Hiếu and his siblings had to move to an NEZ after 1975. Sitting in a park in west Berlin, he calmly described this time without the slightest indication of bitterness:

> That means people—the government brought our family to an area . . . the countryside so we could farm. I'm not clear on whether that was good or not but perhaps one issue was people didn't have experience

with a rural life, and then they were brought there, so they didn't have experience . . . so it was as if they were exiled.

(Tức là người ta—chính phủ đưa gia đình mình đến cái khu . . . quê thôn để mình làm farm, nông trại. Thì chú chưa hiểu rõ đó có tốt không nhưng mà có lẽ là một số cái không tốt là những người ta không có kinh nghiệm về đời sống nông thôn, thế mang người ta đấy . . . thành thử giống như người ta bị đi đấy, Exil.)

Born in South Vietnam in the early 1960s, Hiếu was a teenager when the government relocated him and his surviving family members to an NEZ. Hiếu did not interpret this as a form of persecution but as an agricultural policy that worsened an already fragile economy. This points to the gap between individuals' understandings of persecution versus state policies that target families deemed antirevolutionary.

Hiếu's conviction that life was difficult for everyone further suggests that all migrations are in a sense politically motivated, because people living in effective regimes would be able to survive adequately. That is because "the normal bond between the citizen and the state can be severed in diverse ways . . . [including state] fraility [*sic*]."[71] Political regimes therefore shape people's livelihoods in ways that necessarily reach beyond politics, affecting infrastructure and at times decimating the economy.

Citizens in the north had been pacified by a disciplined authoritarian state; after reunification, the SRV needed to exert similar control over its new southern population. This at times ran counter to the messages of peace that officials offered. For example, immediately after South Vietnamese General Dương Văn Minh capitulated to North Vietnamese Colonel Bùi Tín on April 30, 1975, the latter reportedly told the former, "You have nothing to fear. Between Vietnamese there are no victors and no vanquished. Only the Americans have been beaten. If you are patriots, consider this a moment of joy. The war for our country is over."[72] Despite Bùi's assurances that there would be "no victors and no vanquished," up to 1 million people with ties to the former Southern regime were soon "invited" to reeducation for three days to one month.[73] Widespread throughout communist countries, these prisons

involved forced labor and indoctrination via propaganda under conditions of food scarcity and minimal medical treatment.[74] For RVN officers, government workers, religious leaders, and others with American
ties who reported for reeducation, the days turned into weeks, months,
and years. Many did not survive the prison sentence.

Young Vietnamese men had further reason to fear violence after
1975. By December 1978, tensions between reunified Vietnam and its
Cambodian allies, the Khmer Rouge, boiled over into armed conflict.
Fearing Vietnamese intentions of dominating former Indochina, the
Khmer Rouge began to purge its own soldiers who had been trained
by Vietnamese. The conflict with Cambodia had important socioeconomic and political implications. First, it removed many men from
the labor market.[75] It also incurred the international community's
condemnations against Vietnam.[76] In particular, China leaped to
Cambodia's defense. The resulting tense diplomatic relations between
Vietnam and China spiraled into increasingly antagonistic treatment
of Vietnam's Chinese-origin population. These ethnic Chinese made
up a large proportion of boat refugees fleeing at the end of 1978. Some
300,000 people of Chinese descent resettled in China as a result.[77]

Refugees' exodus resulted from state actions that identified and
punished internal enemies. State persecution took on different forms,
not all of which involved violence or led to impossible living conditions. Some people, such as former RVN officers who were imprisoned, experienced physical and economic persecution. More dreaded
the effects of the three-generation life history or cited the abject economic conditions they endured in post-1975 Vietnam as impelling
their border crossing. Still others feared more deaths on the horizon,
given the looming conflicts with China and Cambodia. Crucially, this
involved a national military draft rather than policies targeting southerners and antirevolutionaries. At least some of those later granted
refugee status abroad were "victims of what might be called nefarious
political routine, a vast category that includes most of the citizens of
illiberal states . . . [but this is different from] those who are singled out
as targets for the willful exercise of extraordinary malevolence on the
part of some agent."[78]

This distinction between general oppression and targeted persecution has been blurry and inconsistent in practice. In the United States, for example, the Jimmy Carter administration treated Southeast Asian refugee claims as group based, in contrast to the individual-based definition of the 1951 UN Convention.[79] Until 2017, Cuban arrivals to the United States also benefited from expedited pathways to residency because of their country of origin.[80] By contrast, Chinese asylum seekers to Australia find their claims routinely denied because forced sterilization under the one-child policy results from "a general law . . . [that] lack[s] the critical nexus between fear and UN Convention grounds that would make them eligible for refugee protection."[81] Whereas the UN definition emphasizes persecution, other entities (such as the Organization of African Unity) recognize that persecution is just one way that the bond between citizen and state can dissolve.[82]

But whether stemming from general oppression or targeted persecution, the SRV's mistreatment of some for their loyalties fueled Southern identity in enduring ways. Southerners I spoke with interpreted the actions of the reunified government as an attack on southernness. They believed so even though the DRV had similarly identified, suppressed, and disciplined ordinary Northerners into submission decades earlier.

The division and reunification of Vietnam expose the unequal effects of state formations: although the creation of separate Vietnamese states forged a shared nationalism, the reunification of these states did not erase competing Northern and Southern nationhoods. This may well be because the principle of ethnic nationalism was not fully accepted.[83] After all, "Vietnam" had only been unified "for the first time in the nineteenth century . . . [and this] had been brief and unsuccessful."[84] Although leaders of both states impressed on citizens the need to reunite with their compatriots across the 17th parallel, Vietnamese-speaking people did not necessarily identify as one people at the turn of the twentieth century, as the chapter's opening quote heeds. This chapter hints at how they eventually would come to do so through repeatedly encountering both states' claims that Vietnam was a divided nation in need of reunification. In later chapters, we explore how the political project of ethnic nationalism would unravel in present-day Berlin. Although border crossings may shape the contour and intensity of people's political identities, they do not necessarily determine its substance.

The same is true of international migration. Tài and Kiều, who transformed from Northerners to Southerners in 1954, would not revert back to simply Vietnamese after crossing borders into West Germany. As the following chapters detail, refugees and their family members would instead carry their Southern identity and politics with them to their adopted homeland. Although border crossings may craft new political configurations, the undoing of these crossings does not equally undo how people experience ethnic nationhood. Nor does it prevent them from drawing on their nationhood as a frame for being in and seeing the world.

Competing Nationhood, Shared Nationalism

At the end of the Second Indochina War in 1975, two separate understandings of Vietnamese nationhood coincided: for northerners, a reunified nation under a communist government; for southerners, a morally superior but militarily defeated, anticommunist nation in exile. But although the narratives of Vietnamese nationhood took on different forms in the context of the Cold War, both states engaged in similar nation-making processes. After 1954, both used the auspices of war and state security to reward loyalty, as when the North sent Nam to study in East Germany and the South sent Kiều to West Germany. Both states took measures to identify, punish, and thwart internal enemies. The North did so with far more success than the South. By mobilizing the state against class traitors like Sơn's landowning family, the DRV effectively disciplined its population into docility. The RVN likewise imprisoned or killed dissenters, but it could not eliminate all groups opposed to the government.

Through bureaucratic practices that marked citizens as enemies or patriots, the Vietnamese states manufactured conflicting versions of Vietnamese national identity. To be sure, it was the North that engaged in expansionist efforts to conquer the South, not the other way around. Nonetheless, this chapter has traced how new forms of nationhood surfaced in the aftermath of state formation, across political regimes that saw themselves as polar opposites.

At the same time that state formation created competing nationhoods, the claim of both states to represent all Vietnamese people in effect advanced a shared nationalism. This politics of ethnic nationalism proclaims that the Vietnamese people should be governed solely by the legitimate Vietnamese state. The discrepancy between peoplehood and politics tells us that the national is not always nationalist, and vice versa. As Phước's earlier remarks suggest, northernness is bound up with communism, the war, and, implicitly, atheism. The national project of the RVN framed Southerners as anticommunist, democracy loving, and religiously diverse. The following pages delve into how Vietnamese contract workers to the Eastern Bloc and refugees to West Germany transported these understandings of Cold War nationhood and nationalism with them across borders, before interrogating how these change along the way.

3 Making Refugees and Contract Workers

JUST TEN YEARS OLD when Vietnam reunified under a one-party social-ist system, Thọ inherited an "anti-revolutionary" background because his father had served in the South Vietnamese army. Thọ understood that as a result, his opportunities to study and find a good job would be curtailed. His already vulnerable position as a child of a Southern soldier was aggravated by the fact that Vietnam continued to be at war with neighboring countries after 1975. Thọ's family expected that he would soon be drafted to fight in Cambodia, where he would likely perish. Because their family could afford passage on a boat for only one person, Thọ fled by himself at age fourteen.

Speaking slowly and deliberately in an office that had closed for the day, Thọ recounted his escape in June 1979. He spelled out his reasons for fleeing Vietnam matter-of-factly: he could not envision a future for himself there. Because his escape had long since concluded, Thọ did not exude the fearfulness that he surely felt at the time. His detached exterior began to unravel, however, as he recalled watch-ing someone steering a ship masterfully on the night of his escape. Forgetting himself, he thought at the time, *I have to go home and tell mom about this* (*Cái này phải về kể cho mẹ nghe*). But he collected himself immediately, the weight of his course sinking in. Thọ realized that he "would never be able to return. From that moment on [he] could not cry" (*Không bao giờ quay trở về được. Từ lúc đó không khóc được*). Thọ paused from his story to invoke the lyrics of a mournful diasporic Vietnamese song: "The boat that carries me away will take me back home" (*Tàu đưa ta đi tàu sẽ đón ta hồi hương*). But as Thọ boarded his boat that summer night and watched the land fade into the background, he mourned a homeland to which he never expected to return.

Measuring sixty-five feet long and ten feet wide, the boat that carried Thọ from his homeland had a maximum capacity of three hundred people. He later learned that six hundred were onboard. During the journey, a Thai fishing vessel stalked their rickety boat for a day. Laughing dryly, Thọ recalled that when the boat caught up to them, the Thais claimed they had simply wanted to offer the refugees some assistance. Thọ suspected that the Thais meant to raid the ship, but changed their minds because of the sheer number of people they would have had to overpower to do so. He had reason to doubt their intentions: piracy in Southeast Asia had been long-standing, and the rate had mushroomed with the exodus of boat people in their often unseaworthy vessels.[1] When Thọ's boat approached Malaysia days later, it was promptly repelled.[2] A week after departing Vietnam, the boat docked at Kuku Island, Indonesia.

Thọ had survived a treacherous journey that would claim numerous lives throughout the 1980s and leave others with trauma from pirate attacks and survivor's guilt. But his future remained uncertain. As hundreds of thousands of people risked their lives on the seas, the UN Secretary-General called on countries to respond to the asylees' plight. To discourage Southeast Asian countries from pushing back boats, the UN sought to swiftly resettle these de facto refugees in third countries.[3] In the midst of this scramble, Thọ learned that he would be relocated to West Germany. Some people he knew in the Indonesian camp expressed their horror about this decision because West Germany was "so close to Communists, so they were scared" (*Ở sát cộng sản quá họ cũng sợ*). They feared a repeat of the communist invasion and victory that they had left behind in Vietnam. Not only did democratic West Germany border communist the East, but the city of West Berlin was entirely encircled by the East. However, Thọ reasoned that he had escaped not knowing if he would survive. Whatever lay ahead would surely be better than being sent back to Vietnam.

Migration scholars refer to the circumstances under which people such as Thọ leave their homelands as their context of exit.[4] These circumstances may be menacing, as Thọ and other refugees experienced. Perhaps because their departures from Vietnam proved so uncertain, the refugees I met often offered lengthy answers to my opening question, "Can you tell me how you [or your parents] came to this country?" (*[Bác/cô/chú/anh/chị/em] có thể nói cho [con/em/chị] biết thế nào [bác/cô/chú/anh/chị/em] đã đến nước này được không?*)[5] In contrast, people who went abroad through more orderly channels, such as formal labor recruitment, did not dwell on their exit in the same way.

Ngọc Lan, whose context of exit from Vietnam could not have been more dissimilar from Thọ's, recounted her departure without the slightest hint of suspense. Born in North Vietnam in 1963, she was two years older than Thọ. Whereas insecurity characterized his journey, excitement marked hers. She prepared to leave Vietnam for the first time in 1981 as part of a contingent of contract workers sent to East Germany and other socialist states. Whereas Thọ anticipated hardship in his life because his father was a Southern soldier, Ngọc Lan's parents both were members of the Worker's Party of Vietnam (which became the Communist Party of Vietnam). Because they were party members, Ngọc Lan was able to go abroad to work. People so desired such an opportunity that they mobilized their connections in the party, military, or other networks and at times paid bribes to secure contracts.[6] By 1986, roughly twelve thousand Vietnamese would go to East Germany, concentrating in East Berlin as well as cities such as Dresden and Leipzig. A larger second wave would go there between 1987 and 1989.

Ngọc Lan anticipated an exciting but ultimately straightforward time living and working abroad. Unlike Thọ, she was not gripped with uncertainty about her departure from her homeland. The East

German and Vietnamese governments arranged every aspect of her travel. For her part, she needed to pass a medical exam to prove herself physically fit to represent the Socialist Republic of Vietnam abroad. She did not need to say tearful good-byes to her loved ones, bribe officers for passage onto the vessel that would take her away, or flee under the cover of night. While attending school in North and then reunified Vietnam, Ngọc Lan had learned that "everything socialist is good" (*Alles, was sozialistisch ist, ist gut*). Trusting this, she welcomed the opportunity to acquire skills abroad that she hoped to bring back to aid in Vietnam's postwar reconstruction. Filled with "pride in and gratitude to the Vietnamese government" (*tự hào và rất là cảm ơn chính quyền Việt Nam*) for making her voyage possible, Ngọc Lan expected to repatriate after her contract ended. Unlike Thọ in his interview, Ngọc Lan did not linger on the context of her exit. She jumped instead to her life once she set foot on East German soil.

Although Thọ and Ngọc Lan represent quintessential refugees and contract workers (southerner versus northerner, persecuted versus rewarded, turbulent flight versus organized departure), people's regions of origin and experiences with state violence did not always map cleanly onto their migration pathways. As we learned in Chapter 2, people who had been born in northern Vietnam before the country divided also identified as Southerners and would eventually flee by boat. Some who would later receive refugee recognition had not experienced persecution. Others had time to plan their journeys. Still others living in the north also fled Vietnam after 1975, but were far less likely to be recognized as refugees.[7]

Because East Germany initiated a bilateral labor agreement with reunified Vietnam, contract workers came from throughout the country, including the south. In fact, the same northern provinces that produced asylees to Hong Kong in the late 1970s would also provide contract workers to the Eastern Bloc.[8] Among the ranks of contract workers were those who had directly experienced state violence but would ultimately be classified as economic migrants, including Sơn, whom we met in the previous chapter. This chapter therefore affirms that the "[migrant/refugee] binary is a legal fiction because everything we know about people who decide to move suggests that their motivations and lived experiences are far more complicated than any binary . . . can fully encompass."[9]

At the point of their departures from Vietnam, Thọ and Ngọc Lan differed from each other not primarily in their individual traits but in how they were allowed to leave. Neither had specialized skills, experience, or knowledge that would qualify them as human capital migrants, though it required some money for Thọ and connections for Ngọc Lan to be able to leave. Having grown up in a postwar economy in tatters, neither had studied at a university or had spoken a word of German when they left Vietnam. But in contrast to Thọ, Ngọc Lan could reasonably expect to survive her journey. She knew to which country she was headed. Both had strong ideas about when they would return to Vietnam: for Thọ, likely never; for Ngọc Lan, certainly.

How did these divergent experiences take shape once Thọ, Ngọc Lan, and refugees and contract workers like them reached their respective host countries? The journey out of Vietnam for refugees like Thọ began with indeterminacy, which ebbed as they started their new lives. For contract workers like Ngọc Lan, it began full of hope, which later waned when the Eastern Bloc dissolved. Both refugees and contract workers would experience waves of joy and despair, contingency, and possibility, though at different moments in their departures and time abroad. First, though, they would find paradise on both sides of the Berlin Wall.

Refugees Welcome

Western countries, including the Federal Republic of Germany, sought to address the plight of boat people like Thọ through concerted rescue and resettlement efforts. Western countries granted protection to Vietnamese and, more broadly, Southeast Asian boat people in part because of their geopolitical significance. In the United States, the figure of the refugee provided the "(re)cuperation of American identities" after a devastating military loss in the Vietnam War.[10] Such "calculated kindness" often underlines humanitarian operations,[11] as was true of Cuban arrivals to the United States after the Cuban Revolution in 1959.[12] Though shouldering the majority of Vietnamese refugee resettlement, the United States pushed West Germany and its other allies to resettle refugees as well. (See Figure 3.1.)

In hindsight, it is remarkable that Thọ and some ten thousand Vietnamese received status as contingent refugees despite the prevailing sentiment that West Germany was not a country of immigration. The government insisted this even as millions of foreign citizens lived and worked there.[13] The FRG confronted this apparent contradiction by regarding guest workers from Turkey and other European countries as a temporary exception to the idea of (West) Germany for Germans. Guest worker programs explicitly excluded non-Europeans, and lawmakers worked "actively to prevent employers from recruiting workers from Asian and African countries and to make sure that such individuals would not become settled in West Germany."[14]

Yet the federal government afforded Vietnamese people special status because of both the highly publicized crisis they faced at sea and the legacy of twentieth-century German history. In response to its Nazi past, West Germany went above and beyond the UN Convention's call for granting asylum to guaranteeing the right to asylum.[15] This right included substantial welfare benefits even before individuals successfully claimed asylum. It remained enshrined in the German Basic Law until 1993, by which point reunified Germany had accepted more refugees than all other western European countries combined.[16]

Although Thọ's context of exit from Vietnam was stormy, his context of reception in West Germany was largely positive. These contexts include "the policies of the receiving government, the character of the host labor market, and the features of [migrants'] own ethnic communities."[17] Regarding the first dimension, Thọ arrived in West Berlin in early autumn 1979 with robust government support. Refugees first received humanitarian passports and temporary residence. Thọ first went to live with forty-nine other unaccompanied minors, most of them boys. They stayed in Wannsee, a wealthy area of southwest Berlin. Thọ's accommodations boasted a large garden and tennis court,

Figure 3.1 "Arrival of Refugees from Vietnam and Cambodia in Frankfurt 1979 (Ankunft von Flüchtlingen aus Vietnam und Kambodscha in Frankfurt/ Main 1979)." Source: Engelbert Reineke/Bundesregierung, B 145 Bild-00138434. Reprinted with permission.

which cheered up the children despite their poverty and separation from their families. Thọ's eyes twinkled as he recalled German children at school asking where he lived. When he told them Wannsee, they responded, astonished, that his parents must be really wealthy. The unaccompanied minors had a caretaker, a translator, and teachers who came each day to tutor them in German before they could start attending a local school. After six months, Thọ went to live with a host family to further his integration. Eventually he sponsored his parents and siblings under the age of eighteen from Vietnam. They all benefited from the resettlement structure in place and had clear pathways to West German citizenship.

Refugees' options to naturalize were a sharp break from German legal precedence. Unlike the United States and other countries that grant birthright citizenship (*jus soli*), West Germany conferred blood-right citizenship (*jus sanguinis*). This created a situation in which multiple generations of Turkish Germans, for instance, lived in West

Germany without access to citizenship. Only in 2000 did Germany
begin to recognize jus soli, but even then, under strict conditions. The
arrival of Vietnamese in West Germany thus challenged the country's
ethnocultural conception of citizenship.[18]

Not only did federal and state governments provide assistance to
refugee arrivals, but civil society also rallied to welcome them.[19] Public figures, journalists, and volunteers launched highly successful aid
campaigns on behalf of the boat people. This included private citizens who chartered a ship, *Cap Anamur*, to rescue overcrowded boats
in the South China Sea. Because the *Cap Anamur* sailed under the
West German flag, the government was "formally obligated to take the
shipwrecked refugees."[20] (See Figure 3.2.)

Thọ alluded to this public support for refugees, given Germans'
reluctance to embrace outsiders. Specifically, he recalled his foster
mother's advice when he contemplated accepting a job offer in a small
village outside West Berlin. Herself a former refugee from Eastern Europe, Thọ's foster mother warned that Germans viewed strangers the
way they did unfamiliar food—with suspicion. "But if they like us,"
he evoked her words, "then they really care. . . . When they meet us
and don't know who we are, they hate us. . . . From fear it becomes
hatred." (*Nếu mà họ thích mình rồi thì họ thương mình lắm. Khi mà họ
gặp mình mà họ không biết mình là ai, họ ghét mình. . . . Từ cái sợ đến
cái ghét.*) Thọ did not consider Germans racist. To his mind, Germans
were simply afraid of unfamiliar things. He felt that this required new
arrivals to be open (*cởi mở*) for Germans to reciprocate. Like many
other refugees, Thọ would indeed find German natives open toward
him and would ultimately form deep relationships that endured for
decades.

Thọ arrived in West Germany in an era marked by economic
prosperity, the second dimension of contexts of reception. In part,
West Germany owed its economic miracle to the vast sums of foreign money being infused into the last frontier between Western Europe and socialism. But whereas young arrivals saw opportunities to
reinvent themselves, older arrivals at times struggled to master the
German language. Some found, to their dismay, that they could not

Figure 3.2 "Vietnamese Boat People arrive with the ship *Cap Anamur* on 27 July 1982 in Hamburg." Source: Sven Simon/Associated Press Images. Reprinted with permission.

convert their qualifications from Vietnam into similar jobs in their host country.[21] On the whole, however, refugees and their family members secured steady employment by the late 1980s.[22]

Migrants' coethnic communities are the third dimension of contexts of reception, after the policies of the receiving government and the labor market. When Thọ arrived in West Germany, few Vietnamese had lived there. The sixteen hundred who preceded him largely came as international students on scholarships from South Vietnam.[23] This was true of Kiều, whom we met in Chapter 2. Students like her received refugee passports when South Vietnam fell. Like other countries of refugee resettlement, West Germany would disperse refugee arrivals to avoid putting too much strain on any one local government. Refugees who resettled in small towns across West Germany often found themselves the only visible racial minority in the vicinity. On the eve of German reunification, refugees and their family members numbered between 33,000 and 38,000 across the West

German states.[24] On the whole, then, refugees did not benefit from
the same extensive coethnic networks that have come to character-
ize Vietnamese communities across the United States, Canada, and
other countries of resettlement.[25] In other instances, these networks
provide in-language resources, access to information about jobs and
housing, and affective support. In West Germany, the state and civil
society stepped in to facilitate refugee integration.

Socialist Workers of the World Unite

It was not only refugees who had the advantage of a positive government and labor market reception, however. Until the fall of the Berlin Wall, so did contract workers. In contrast with the West German
infrastructure of refugee resettlement, Eastern Bloc governments did
not seek to integrate contract workers. Nevertheless, Vietnamese contract workers felt welcomed by their host governments and had economic opportunities far superior to what they had known in Vietnam.
Viewing their lives abroad through a "dual frame of reference,"[26] many
contract workers considered East Germany a "paradise."[27]

The label of contract worker, like with that of refugee, exists
through the negotiations of states.[28] In 1980, Vietnam signed a labor
agreement that would result in 70,000 to 80,000 workers coming
to East Germany. Vietnam had similar agreements with Bulgaria,
Czechoslovakia, and the Soviet Union, which would see 300,000
Vietnamese working in the Eastern Bloc before the fall of the Soviet
Union.[29] Mirroring West Germany and South Vietnam, East Germany had a long-standing relationship with North Vietnam, having
received and trained Vietnamese students decades before the labor
program began.[30] Proficient in German, these students would return
in the 1980s to serve as group leaders for labor contingents. Workers
who arrived early in the decade also included some higher-skilled migrants than those who would arrive starting in the late 1980s.[31]

Like its Western counterpart, the East German government arranged each aspect of Vietnamese workers' lives abroad. However,
East Germany worked to prevent foreign workers from mingling

with its native population.[32] This practice remains typical of receiving states in temporary migration regimes.[33] New arrivals to East
Berlin, for example, went directly from Berlin-Schönefeld Airport to
their ethnic- and gender-segregated hostels.[34] Ngọc Lan followed the
same procedure, though she was destined for another city. East German authorities promptly confiscated her passport. What they feared
most, she explained, was that contract workers would flee to the West,
as many natives had done, and delegitimize the regime by doing so.
During her contract, Ngọc Lan shared a room with four other young
women who worked in her labor contingent. Recalling that time
decades later, Ngọc Lan shuddered at the living conditions and surveillance to which they were subjected. As with all contract workers,
Ngọc Lan had a coethnic group leader as well as translator to address
her day-to-day concerns. They also discouraged workers from learning German beyond what it took to perform their duties. Nevertheless, Ngọc Lan treasured her newfound freedom to earn money and
be independent.

Ngọc Lan also delighted in what she saw as the emancipation of
German women. She relished hearing about them going to the disco
and drinking, feeling that "German women have an immense freedom" (*phụ nữ Đức có cái Freiheit rất là lớn*).

Despite enforced segregation between native and foreign workers,
East Germans still interacted with Vietnamese. Whereas West German civil society praised Vietnamese refugees as an integration success story, their East German counterpart (as well as the Stasi) hailed
Vietnamese contract workers as diligent workers of the world. Angola,
Cuba, Mozambique, and other socialist solidarity states also sent contract workers to East Germany. It was the Vietnamese, though, who
earned the image of industrious comrades. (See Figure 3.3.)

Like their refugee counterparts, contract workers found their host
state to be a land of plenty. Ngọc Lan entered an East German economy short of labor and contributed to a homeland economy in need
of money to rebuild after a long and costly war. The Vietnamese government initially deducted 15 percent of contract workers' monthly
earnings toward this national reconstruction. By the late 1980s, they

Figure 3.3 Photo, "Cottbus, Vietnamese work in textile combine (Cottbus, Vietnamesen arbeiten im Textilkombinat)," March 1989. Source: Rainer Weisflog/Bundesarchiv, Bild 183-1989-0330-300. Reprinted with permission.

withheld only 12 percent. Contract workers also had ways of earning extra income, including performing services such as laundry and tailoring for Germans.[35] Despite competing state goals of isolation versus integration, then, contract workers' early contexts of reception in East Germany at times mirrored that of refugees in the West.

Yet contract workers and refugees differed from each other in two crucial ways. First, contract workers could not come with their families and had no rights of family reunification. Moreover, authorities discouraged sexual liaisons between foreign and native workers. Women who became pregnant faced the almost certain threat of deportation. This was the case for Ngọc Lan, who had the option to renew her labor contract for another two years. During this time, she fell in love with a German man and went into hiding to give birth to their child. Her circumstances contrasted sharply with that of most other contract workers, who would not experience legal uncertainty until after the fall of the Berlin Wall in 1989.

Second, compared with refugees, contract workers had ethnic social capital, the third dimension of contexts of reception, in spades. Their home and host governments had designed it so, with nearly every moment of contract workers' daily lives being spent around coethnics. Vietnamese concentrated in the same dorms, factories, and cities across East Germany. Although mandatory and taken for granted during the 1980s, these networks would prove crucial to contract workers after the fall of the Berlin Wall in 1989. (See Table 3.1.)

Dual and Triple Frames of Reference

Ngọc Lan and Thọ stepped foot on their respective German soils with what they both experienced as a positive context of reception. They diverged in whether they had access to family reunification rights and extensive coethnic social networks. Yet both appreciated their time abroad on the whole because they compared it with their lives in Vietnam.

Whereas contract workers could compare their lives abroad only with Vietnam, some refugees weighed it against both their experiences in Vietnam and what they observed behind the Iron Curtain. Thọ, for example, had made several trips into East Berlin before the wall fell. West Germans as well as refugees with humanitarian passports could cross into the East, but East Germans and contract workers could not easily venture into the West. Because Thọ's foster father had friends from the East, Thọ was familiar with these border crossings. It was over the course of trips to the East that he met Vietnamese contract workers whose knowledge of the German language he described as completely absent. "Their lives were very hard" (*Họ sống rất là cực*), he recalled. They "went to work, went home, and did not interact with Germans" (*đi làm về họ không có tiếp xúc với người Đức*).

The asymmetry in contract workers' and refugees' frames of reference contributed to both feeling that they had been welcomed well by their respective host governments and labor markets. Like Thọ,

Table 3.1 Migration Trends. Source: Author.

	Refugees	Contract Workers
Demographics		
Age	0+	18 to 35
Sex	More males	More balanced
Beginning wave	1979	1980
Context of reception		
Government		
State goals	Integration	Productivity and isolation
Housing	Dorms, foster families	Ethnic- and gender-segregated dorms
Language training	Minimum six months	Less than three months
Reunification rights	Contingent, largely supported	Only after 1990
Labor market	Strong, difficult to translate credentials	Job conditions superior to Vietnam
Coethnic community	Small, geographically dispersed	Large, geographically concentrated

border crossers across the world move within social fields that connect them with knowledge about the experiences of their coethnics in different receiving countries.[36] But this requires access to information about such coethnics, information that contract workers such as Ngọc Lan largely lacked. She had heard about boat people in the United States and Canada. But she had no idea while living in East Germany that refugees also lived across the border. And just as contract workers and refugees possessed unequal access to information about life on the other side of the Berlin Wall, they would encounter the fall of the wall with unequal weight.

Refugees after the Fall of the "Evil Empire"

Refugees and contract workers were unevenly equipped to deal with the political upheaval that followed the fall of the Berlin Wall on November 9, 1989. News of impending German reunification followed shortly. The Berlin Wall was soon leveled and East Germany reabsorbed into the structure of West Germany. The newly reunified country experienced economic decline as it reintegrated the poorer East. As the epicenter of reunification, the city of Berlin underwent much structural flux.

Yet for the most part, refugees living in reunifying Berlin found their lives relatively unchanged compared to their contract worker coethnics. For those in West Germany, the fall of the Eastern Bloc affirmed their belief that the "Evil Empire" could not persist—though Vietnam remained socialist. Some refugees, like Tín (Chapter 6), would lose their jobs when their companies closed. Their permanent residency or German citizenship, however, protected these refugees from feeling the brunt of the economic and political upheaval.

In the turbulent months following the fall of the Berlin Wall, refugees and contract workers seemed to have overcome homeland divisions. Despite their newfound citizenship, refugees still felt solidarity with contract workers. Refugees were staunch in the belief that they shared with contract workers an unquestionable sense of peoplehood—that they remained members of the same ethnic nation.

Thắm, a southerner who arrived in West Berlin in the 1980s through family reunification for refugees, took this commonality for granted: "There were few Vietnamese [in West Berlin] at the time, and there [in the East] were our countrymen, so we felt love." (*Ở đây ít người Việt Nam lắm, ở đó có người đồng hương thì mình thấy thương.*) Thắms words suggest that she sees ethnic nationhood as something that cannot be dissolved even when refugees have forfeited their Vietnamese citizenship and acquired a West German one. Indeed, Thắm claimed that back then, "Everyone was bringing [contract workers] home, feeding them. . . . At that time there wasn't yet animosity between north and south." (*Ai cũng đem về nhà, cho ăn, cho uống. . . . Lúc đó chưa có kỳ thị giữa nam và bắc.*)

Boosting Thắm claim of widespread camaraderie, some refugees like Thọ halted their studies so that they could fully commit to assisting coethnic contract workers. "When the Berlin Wall fell," Thọ and "people here in the West, everyone welcomed [contract workers]" (*Khi bức tường vừa mới đổ, người bên Tây này, ai cũng đón tất cả*). Thọ began to skip classes and for the next six months devoted his time to translating and arranging shelter for contract workers. He housed upward of thirty people in the three-bedroom home he shared with his family. Thọ would resume his university studies years later, majoring in administration so that he could help Vietnamese people as well as serve as a bridge between Vietnamese and German society.

Beyond providing assistance to contract workers, some Vietnamese border crossers to the West also felt compelled to explain and apologize for the actions of their coethnics to Germans. Compared to Thọ who was a boat person (*thuyền nhân*), his friend Kỳ was a self-styled "plane person" (*phi nhân*) who came to West Germany through family reunification for refugees. Born in South Vietnam in 1967, Kỳ arrived in West Germany in 1983. He lived in a small village far from West Berlin and seldom encountered coethnics. When the Berlin Wall fell, contract workers began to cross over into the West to file for asylum. The police in Kỳ's village soon came to ask him for help translating. His coethnics had caused traffic accidents and been apprehended for drunkenness and public disturbance. Like Thọ, Kỳ felt the strong pull of ethnicity:

> We wanted to rescue our compatriots, why? We already escaped from communism, but now they were fleeing [the fall of] communism so we opened our arms wide [to receive them]. We didn't know who they were, we didn't know if they followed communism or not.
>
> (*Mình muốn cứu được đồng bào của mình tại vì sao? Mình đã trốn chạy cộng sản rồi, mà bây giờ họ cũng trốn chạy thì mình mở vòng tay. Mình không biết người đó là ai, mình không biết người đó theo cộng sản hay không theo cộng sản.*)

Kỳ served a double role as translator and apologist, explaining that contract workers behaved badly because of their circumstances.

Even while defending contract workers to German authorities, however, Kỳ and Thọ noted that these circumstances had begun to damage the reputation of Vietnamese. This hit Thọ when a native coworker asked him if he had time later that day so that they could go assault (the other kind of) Vietnamese together. Thọ and other refugees had painstakingly cultivated an image of their ethnic group as grateful and outstanding German citizens. The arrival of contract workers after the fall of the Berlin Wall jeopardized that.

In one sense, this racial lumping by Germans activated a pan-Vietnamese solidarity.[37] Kỳ, for example, defended contract workers' actions as a consequence of their uncertain legal statuses after the fall of the Berlin Wall. By and large, the refugees I spoke with did not recall publicly distancing themselves from contract workers for Germans' sake.

Refugees and their family members did, however, begin to privately distance themselves from contract workers. Coethnic relationships began to sour even for refugees who were willing to receive contract workers into their homes. Thắm stressed that in her case, this was because of the contract workers' "vices" (*tệ nạn*). The contract workers Thắm housed made expensive calls to Vietnam. They complained that she was cheap for turning down the radiator. The last straw was when one of them made a pass at (*anmachen*) her husband.

Other female refugees reported similar negative experiences with helping contract workers, often around the same themes that painted northern contract worker women as sexually aggressive and manipulative. One person who discussed this at length was Kiều, the northern-born Southerner who was studying in West Germany when South Vietnam fell (Chapter 2). Kiều's mother admonished her not to house contract worker women no matter how much they pleaded. Kiều stressed that if you bring a snake into your home, a man could not help but succumb to her charms. Southerners therefore juxtaposed how they viewed northern women with the virtues they assumed southerners radiated—this, despite documented polygamy, infidelity, and concubinage in the South.[38]

Although exaggerated, these hypersexualized descriptions of contract worker women underscored a real sex imbalance in the two migration streams. Boat refugees tended to be male. When females risked the journeys at sea, they tended to be accompanied by male relatives. By contrast, women formed a bigger share of the contract workforce, though they still remained a minority.[39] As Thọ and Kỳ both stressed, the arrival of contract worker women from the East alleviated the otherwise bleak prospects confronting Vietnamese male bachelors in the West. But in reunifying Berlin, romantic relationships between female contract workers and male refugees appeared to some as a threat to the integrity of the South Vietnamese family.

Vietnamese religious institutions also navigated this tension between refugees' genuine ethnonational solidarity with contract workers versus their possessiveness over the spaces that they had had built in West Berlin. The fledgling Linh Thứu Pagoda played a key role in organizing to help contract workers. As we explore in a later chapter, lay followers aided from a view of Buddhism as anticommunist sanctuary. They reported gathering clothes, providing housing, translating paperwork, and generally helping contract workers who wanted to file for asylum.[40] Yet as Kiều recalled, some refugee disciples bristled at the extent of these solidarity efforts: "Why are you bringing communists into your homes, into our pagoda" (*Tại sao dẫn việt cộng vào nhà, vào chùa*)? Hence, some refugees experienced these coethnic dynamics from the very beginning as tinged with politics. Contract workers, however, had more pressing concerns.

Contract Workers in Paradise Lost

Contract workers felt the consequences of German reunification with force, affirming that "the migrant/refugee binary may be a fiction, but it is powerful, enduring, and deeply consequential one."[41] For some years after 1989, tens of thousands of workers lived in uncertainty. They had no residency rights and few ways of earning a lawful wage as former East German companies fired them. For former contract workers, German reunification ushered in, "above all else, insecurity."[42] Faced with uncertainty about the future, some turned to selling illicit cigarettes to make ends meet. This led to a stigma against Vietnamese as "cigarette mafia" (*Zigarettenmafia*).[43] Germany eventually deported seven thousand Vietnamese for illicit cigarette trading.[44] When German political parties spoke about cigarette mafia, they referred almost exclusively to Vietnamese.[45] The image of Vietnamese as mafia persists today in signs around eastern Berlin warning people not to purchase illicit cigarettes, which purportedly fund terrorism and other nefarious activities.

Living in a northern port city, Ngọc Lan also witnessed the rise in crimes that Kỳ and Thọ lamented. Vietnamese gang activity made headlines, coethnics being the primary victims of violence and murder.[46] Then in 1992, racist mobs burned several apartments where Vietnamese workers had lived. To their horror, sadness, (later) anger, and sense of betrayal, contract workers like Ngọc Lan considered this a turning point in their relationship with Germans.

As the federal government sought to deport Vietnamese contract workers, their context of reception turned decisively hostile.[47] Some workers began to avoid public transportation out of fear of xenophobic attacks.[48] Huệ, a northern contract worker, recalled encountering people on the street who would shout,

You "go back to Vietnam. Fijis." They called Vietnamese Fijis. . . . They
demanded money and cigarettes . . . and if you didn't [give it to them],
they messed with you. . . . They pinned you down completely, took your
money, took all sorts of things. They just left your papers alone. . . . I
only had with me five, ten marks and some cigarettes [at a time].

(*Mày về "ab [nach] Vietnam" đi. "Fidschi." Việt Nam nó gọi là "Fidschi" . . . nó bảo có tiền có thuốc cho nó . . . không thì nó quậy. . . . Nó đè
hết người, nó lấy tiền, lấy các thứ. Chỉ có giấy tờ nó không lấy thôi . . . để
trong ví chỉ có lăm đồng, mười đồng với bao thuốc.*)[49]

Huệ lost her job shortly after the Berlin Wall fell. She needed proof of
housing to be able to stay in reunifying Germany, but many people
would not rent to Vietnamese.[50]

Caught between a home country that would not issue them a return visa and a host country committed to expelling them,[51] contract
workers' uncertain futures echoed that of refugees from the decade
before. Although Huệ decided to stay, many of her coworkers repatriated to Vietnam. Anticipating the transition to a market economy,
the government began to offer an incentive of DM 3,000 to contract
workers to return (roughly $1,735 in December 1999). For perspective,
Vietnam's capita GDP that year was $375. The promise of severance
pay, together with the threatening reality of deportations, meant that
the number of Vietnamese contract workers dropped steeply from
sixty thousand in 1989 to only twenty-one thousand a year later.[52]
From 1990 to 1995, however, Vietnam refused to accept involuntary
returnees who had applied for asylum. Vietnam is not unique in taking this course of action: during World War II, countries of origin routinely denied entry to deportees.[53] Across the decades these examples
spanned, the consequences remained the same—the unwanted did
not know where they would end up, how they would feed themselves,
and what the ramifications would be for their loved ones left behind.

People who repatriated did not always remain in Vietnam, soon
realizing that the DM 3,000 did not last or that they had become
unaccustomed to and increasingly dissatisfied with the Vietnamese
government during their time abroad. This was the case for Minh, a

northerner who came to a Soviet allied country as a contract worker. The country he went to, though "not as developed as East Germany," still "had a sense of culture" (*có nền văn hóa*). It did not restrict news to the extent that Vietnam did. When Minh repatriated in the late 1980s, he found that even his relatively high salary as an engineer could not support his family. He saw this as a failure of the Vietnamese state and began to write critically against the regime. In the early 1990s, Minh left Vietnam for Russia and from there made his way to Germany clandestinely. He registered in an asylum camp in Germany and successfully claimed refugee status. Minh was an exception, however. The German government granted asylum to only 1 percent of an estimated eight to twelve thousand applications.[54] Of the world's estimated refugee population, fewer than 1 percent successfully resettle each year.[55] This makes the chances of refugee resettlement "like winning the lottery."[56] Yet host governments still need to sort out the challenge posed by the remaining 99 percent.

To resolve ambiguity around the status of remaining former contract workers, the reunified German government passed the 1993 right-to-stay legislation. This allowed workers who had arrived before 1982 to apply for long-term visas on the condition that they withdraw their asylum applications. People intending to stay needed proof of social security contributions, a place to live, and German-language competence. Those who applied unsuccessfully for asylum received "toleration status" (*Duldung*), a form of "liminal legality" that was "merely a suspension of deportation and that translate[d] into a highly uncertain legal status."[57] Germany later broadened this right-to-stay legislation in 1997, providing amnesty for a larger number of people. Roughly 10 percent of Vietnamese workers acquired permanent residency this way, and only those privileged few could access rights such as family reunification.[58]

Few contract workers fared better than Trinh, whom we met in Chapter 1. Having been abroad only a few months before the Berlin Wall fell, Trinh hired a guide to help her surreptitiously cross the border into Germany. She filed for asylum in a camp near Frankfurt, and while awaiting the outcome of her case, she began to take integration classes. By 1992, she landed a job at a German company. During these turbulent times, Trinh met her future husband, Nghĩa, also a northern contract worker who had crossed over from the Eastern Bloc. Trinh gave birth to the couple's first child in 1994 while their statuses remained indeterminate. Every moment, she "feared being forced to go back" (sợ là bị về). They scrimped and saved money so that were the family to receive a deportation order, they could resume their lives in Vietnam with a nest egg. Participating in anticommunist protests as a ruse to bolster her asylum claims, Trinh cautiously planned for a future in Germany.

Meanwhile, the German government sought to expel its remaining contract worker population through diplomatic channels. It committed DM 100 million to Vietnam in 1994 in return for the latter to accept repatriated workers. Caught between states unilaterally negotiating over their future, Vietnamese former contract workers would mobilize in protest. (See Figure 3.4.)

Germany and Vietnam would reach a readmission agreement in 1995, but actual repatriation numbers fell short of stated targets: three thousand out of more than thirteen thousand in 1995.[59] Trinh, her husband, and their baby were among those who would escape such sweeps. She received her deportation order in 1998, but a lawyer encouraged her to try to regularize her status through an amendment to the right-to-stay legislation. Trinh technically did not meet the requirements because she gave birth to a child on German soil in 1994, not 1993. Mercifully, officials in the town where Trinh had been living proved lenient. After years of status uncertainty, Trinh and her family at last legalized.

Diverging Contexts, Converging Outcomes

Refugees faced despair that turned into hope after they started their new lives in West Germany, while contract workers moved from optimism to increasing anguish as the Eastern Bloc dissolved. The contexts of reception for both types of migrants changed over time,[60] mirroring each other like ships passing in the night. Contexts of reception

Figure 3.4 "Around 200 Vietnamese, among them Dinh Quan Khanh, who
came to the GDR eight years ago as a contract worker, demonstrated on
Tuesday afternoon, November 28, 1995, in Erfurt for the right to stay for
2000 Vietnamese in Thuringia" (Etwa 200 Vietnamesen, unter ihnen auch
Dinh Quan Khanh, der vor acht Jahren als Vertragsarbeiter in die DDR kam,
demonstrieren am Dienstag nachmittag, 28. November 1995, in Erfurt fuer
das Bleiberecht von 2000 Vietnamese in Thueringen). Source: Jens Meyer/
Associated Press. Reprinted with permission.

can thus turn discriminatory toward migrants during economic and
political crises,[61] as Vietnamese contract workers experienced in the
late 1980s. Once seen as workers in socialist solidarity, Vietnamese
soon became the targets of xenophobic violence and expulsion efforts.
Stigma against Vietnamese border crossers did not remain within
the territory of the former East either. Instead, negative labels circulated into the west. This spoiled how natives there saw Vietnamese
border crossers as well, as when Thọ's coworker suggested they go

batter Vietnamese former contract workers for sport. That refugees and contract workers arrived in divided Germany under formally different auspices did not fully distinguish them. Their reputations were instead linked, in the eyes of both Vietnamese and native Germans, by a shared ethnic nationhood.

Though refugees and contract workers faced diverging contexts of reception, this did not necessarily lead them to dissimilar life outcomes.[62] Rather, contract workers had a wider range of outcomes. Yet many refugees and contract workers would attain the same levels of proficiency in German, employment, and legal status. Refugees like Thọ and their family members like Kỳ, once they completed their university studies, often went into solidly middle-class professions. Thọ and Kỳ were living in Berlin by the time I met them in 2016, Thọ working as a public servant and Kỳ as a medical professional. Other refugees went on to complete professional degrees and largely found stable employment. Those who did not could still rely on the protections of the German welfare state. Former contract worker Ngọc Lan later completed her education and worked as an interpreter. Like Thọ, she poured her efforts into bridging Vietnamese and German interests, lending her expertise to government integration projects. Huệ, who border-crossed much later than Thọ and Ngọc Lan, never did master the German language. She had already retired by the time we met, however, and received enough support from the German government to live comfortably in eastern Berlin. By 2016, Trinh and her husband, Nghĩa, operated a business in east Berlin. They lived there with their children, who were German citizens.

Even as they position themselves as opposites, Vietnamese people from different migration streams to Germany have had their share of common experiences. Today, refugees and contract workers as well as their children are widely considered successful—if invisible— minorities.[63] The contexts under which they left Vietnam and arrived abroad shaped how they experienced German reunification but by no means fated them to contradictory paths. It did, however, crystallize for them the Cold War binaries of contract worker versus refugee, communist versus anticommunist, Northerner versus Southerner.

By crossing borders, Vietnamese refugees and contract workers taught themselves and native Germans about national differences. Arriving as legally recognized refugees, individuals like Thọ offered West Germany a vision of how foreigners could become German. By securing employment and living as upright citizens, refugees could repay their debt to West Germany.[64] Arriving as contract workers, individuals like Ngọc Lan briefly bolstered the Eastern Bloc's claims to internationalism and Third World solidarity. Refugees' and contract workers' diverging migration pathways also solidified for them certain understandings of belonging to or rejection of Vietnam. To German natives as well as Vietnamese border crossers, refugees were aligned with anticommunist West Germany and fallen South Vietnam. Similarly, contract workers were associated with the Eastern Bloc, communist Vietnam, and the assumed failings of both. International migration therefore "provided the overall setting for the recognition of difference, the subsequent coding of that difference in national terms, and the dissemination of ideas related to the interpretation of that difference."[65] Border crossings hence reflected and shaped everyday Vietnamese people's understandings of their ethnic nation. This point bears repeating in the following chapter, which centers on how people see and talk about shared ethnic nationhood and nationalism on an everyday level.

4

Ranking the Ethnic Nation

I PROPOSE TURNING OFF THE VOICE RECORDER as my conversation with Liên begins to intensify. A northern woman in her mid-thirties, Liên heard about my study through our mutual friend, Xuân, an international student in her early twenties. Liên and Xuân come from the same northern city of Hai Phong. Curious about my (south) Vietnamese American background, Liên invites me over for dinner with her and Xuân. Petite and wearing a T-shirt and pajamas when we arrive, Liên pops her head out to greet us as we enter through her front door. At the end of the hallway sits Long, a stout man wearing a black sleeveless shirt that exposes his arm tattoos. Liên introduces him as a family friend. Also home are two boys: the first is Liên's stepson, a teenager with dyed blond hair; the second, Liên's toddler, who sits entranced watching the movie *Madagascar*. The room we are in operates as living room, dining room, and bedroom, where Liên, her husband, stepson, and son all sleep.

Liên came to Germany in the early 2000s as a marriage migrant. (Only later do I make the connection that her first husband was the elderly White man in a framed photo on her shelf.) During her first few years in Berlin, Liên interacted only with her husband and German coworkers. She did not have many exchanges with Vietnamese people.

74

After her first husband died, Liên married a recent migrant who is also from her hometown in northern Vietnam. She emphasizes that they avoid coethnics, however, aside from three families they know from back home.

Liên was not the first person to note that she avoided other Vietnamese border crossers. Many who said this came from the north. They also often used the same word to describe the coethnics they tried to avoid: *complicated (phức tạp)*. When pressed, many would point to actions they did not want to be associated with, such as illicit border crossings, black market activity, and general law breaking. These stereotypes reflect the challenging realities many contract workers faced after the fall of the Berlin Wall (Chapter 3).

Today, Vietnamese border crossers use these stereotypes to explain behaviors that people supposedly adopted in Vietnam as a way to survive in an authoritarian state. Liên shared this belief that living in a corrupt system made people desperate—desperate enough that as a young woman, she married a man more than twice her age so that she could go abroad and send remittances back to her family. Liên found conditions in Vietnam so unbearable that she needed to leave; "otherwise, no one wants to leave their homeland."[1] Becoming increasingly animated while talking about Vietnam, Liên declares matter-of-factly that she left because "of course, a capitalist society is always better than a socialist one, right?" (*Thì đương nhiên xã hội tư bản lúc nào cũng tốt hơn xã hội chủ nghĩa rồi, đúng không?*) Leaning in, she asks, "Can I be honest with you?" (*Chị nói thật với em nhé?*) I offer to turn off the voice recorder, to which she consents almost distractedly, before citing her specific grievances against the Vietnamese government.

Frankly, Liên asserts, she prefers the South Vietnamese yellow flag with three red stripes (*cờ vàng ba sọc đỏ*) over the red flag of the Socialist Republic of Vietnam. Liên's husband, Hải, arrives home and enters the room at this moment. We introduce ourselves and he asks where I'm from in Vietnam. When I reply Ho Chi Minh City (formerly Saigon), Hải responds casually that he likes southerners. As we gather on the floor for dinner, Hải remarks that if "the South had won the war, we [Vietnam] would be like Singapore today," economically and socially developed. He then poses a riddle: "One Vietnamese is better than one Japanese, but three Vietnamese cannot beat three Japanese. Why?" At my hesitation, Long, the family friend, answers, "There's no solidarity" (*Không có đoàn kết*). When I ask why they think so, Hải explains that "some things are just too deep in people's personalities, in their beings." Some people simply cannot be decent, he offers.

Mirroring his wife earlier, Hải starts to seethe about the Vietnamese Embassy in Berlin. "Honestly I want to kill them" (*Nói thiệt là anh muốn giết họ*), he says, pained. If he had German citizenship, Hải declares, he would "curse in their faces. They are the lowest of the low, robbing people. But the Vietnamese Consulate in Frankfurt," he points out, "is completely different. Why? Because the people here [in Berlin] are communists."

Hải's objections to the Vietnamese Embassy demonstrates how border crossers map politics onto geography: communists in the east and democrats in the west. Yet Consulate workers in Frankfurt are also citizens of the Vietnamese socialist state. But to Hải, the Consulate's location in west Germany counteracts the communism that he associates with the east. Hải and his wife, Liên, have melded the west with democracy and freedom in their minds and the east with the absence of these defining traits.

In similar fashion, Hải and Liên have come to rank Vietnamese from different regions of origin along a continuum of free to unfree, good to bad. In this national hierarchy, southerners are the top echelon. These include refugees and their family members who came to West Germany and other Western liberal democracies. Liên and Hải rank northerners—including themselves—below southerners.

This hierarchy of Vietnameseness is correlated with membership in Germany and inversely related to membership in Vietnam. By belonging to Germany rather than Vietnam, southerners demonstrate the virtues of Vietnameseness. By belonging not to Germany but to Vietnam, northerners embody its vices. For Liên and Hải, this includes northerners who have naturalized into German citizenship but still carry the invisible scars of growing up under communism.

Hải and Liên's ranking reveals that the ethnic nation is something people talk about and with. In doing so, they bring the nation into being. Vietnamese border crossers in Berlin center the nation both "as the object of talk" and "as an unselfconscious disposition about the national order of things."[2] People like Liên and Hải draw on understandings of the unequal nation to express their worldviews on topics that are not inherently national, from economic hardship to corruption and friendships.

Where the previous two chapters traced how border crossings created the categories of Northerner and Southerner, contract worker and refugee, this chapter turns to how Vietnamese people in Berlin deploy these identities as perspectives on the world.[3] It does so through a deep dive into how Liên and Hải draw on regional, ethnic, and national language in "identifying [themselves] and others, construing situations, explaining behavior, imputing interests, framing complaints, telling stories, etc."[4] This chapter centers narratively on one couple, but by and large the Vietnamese border crossers I met affirmed the same broader points. Vietnamese people widely use collective language such as "we," "our country," and "our Vietnamese brothers and sisters" to express shared ethno-nationhood.[5] Yet the ways that they talk about coethnics also reveal that they do not understand ethnic nationhood as an imagined community involving "a deep, horizontal comradeship."[6]

Indeed, the imagined community metaphor misses how membership can become deeply unequal after border crossings. People may experience the nation hierarchically in contexts of civil war, state formations that involve ethnic unmixing, or return migration.[7] But although the war in Vietnam (and Laos and Cambodia) was in many ways a civil war, it was also thought of and officially referred to as the Anti-American Resistance War for National Salvation (cuộc kháng chiến chống Mỹ cứu nước) (1945–1975). This conflict encompasses earlier anticolonial struggles against the French as well.[8] Liên and Hải's ranking of the ethnic nation, then, is not only about Vietnam's internationalized civil war context but more broadly about the border crossings that they and their homeland experienced.

Vietnamese border crossers understand ethno-nationhood as an "imagined family" that is structured hierarchically.[9] As Liên and Hải's musings suggest, belonging to the imagined family can have negative connotations, implying moral failings. This is because state formation bisected the nation and created internal enemies and heroes (Chapter 2). Vietnamese border crossers carried these unequal homeland memberships with them to Germany, where the paths through which they came shaped their later opportunities for full membership (Chapter 3). The result is a tension between belonging to the homeland and host country. Subsequently, southerners and former refugees who have forfeited Vietnamese citizenship are seen as economically, intellectually, and morally superior. Meanwhile, northerners and former contract workers, many of whom remain Vietnamese citizens, fall short on all accounts because they still belong to the Vietnamese nation-state.

We might well expect legal refugees to draw on these anti-Vietnam narratives to construct their identities in relationship to the homeland and host country;[10] although they certainly do, refugee perspectives are not the focus of this chapter. What is key here is that nonrefugees such as Liên and Hải also valorize refugees and see the latter's exile as a form of purification from a diseased body politic. To Liên and Hải, the nation "is not simply the product of macro-structural forces; it is simultaneously the practical accomplishment of ordinary people engaging in routine activities."[11] For border crossers like them, social and economic activities, big and small, come to reveal the inner rankings of the ethnic nation.

Border crossers rank the ethnic nation not only when they are around coethnic border crossers; they also do so in the presence of natives from various backgrounds. This chapter delves into three settings where this ranking takes place: families, workplaces, and community spaces. It follows Liên and Hải as they talk about the ethnic nation in the intimate setting of their home, documenting some of the couple's domestic disputes. It further shadows Hải at his workplace at a nail salon, grappling with how he experiences his national membership as economic burden. This is also true for his wife: in both of their minds, they are deprived because they belong to a poor, corrupt state. Finally, this chapter revisits the themes of difficult migration routes, challenging socioeconomic outlooks, and family tensions through a social work conference on Vietnamese migrants in Berlin. From these vantage points, we see how Vietnamese border crossers challenge "the idea of a nation defined in the singular . . . [demonstrating instead] a plurality of understandings of nation."[12] Border crossers like Liên and Hải envision a plural nation in which people from different regions all belong, but to varying degrees. In their vision of this plural nation, it is specifically northerners who cause social problems such as black-market dealings (Chapter 3).

Transplanting Disadvantage

Liên and Hải exemplify how northerners' migrations both stem from and exacerbate their already difficult lives. Because of lack of op-portunities available to them in Vietnam, Liên and Hải left through channels less established than those for refugee, labor, or, increas-ingly, student migration. In the early 2000s, twenty-three-year-old Liên married a German man twice her age to improve her family's financial situation. She described this as her first "sacrifice" (*hy sinh*). Fortune smiled on her, however, because her husband was kind. He insisted on accompanying her to work and picking her up each day so that she would feel safe in her new surroundings. Shortly after Liên migrated to Germany, though, her husband fell ill, and Liên spent the remainder of his days nursing him. She then sacrificed her comfort a second time to marry her current husband, Hải, who does not have legal status in Germany. With her first husband, Liên lived in a 100 square meter (roughly 1,000 square feet) apartment for two. Now she lives with three other people in a 30 square meter (roughly 320 square feet) space that offers no privacy. Indeed, Liên speaks in hushed tones about her discontent with this living situation as Hải bellows into the phone in the adjacent kitchen.

Hải sees his migration pathway as necessary because of the national membership he acquired by accident of birth. Life was grueling in

Vietnam, Hải explained, and so he had to leave. He tried to do so twice with fake papers. When he finally succeeded, he came to Germany and had to use someone else's name to be able to work. He pays thousands of euros each year for this service. Visibly distressed, Hải describes knowingly buying cheap clothes from a man who trains children to steal for him. Hải also used to sell illicit cigarettes before he started his current job. "Back then, if someone didn't come home from selling by nightfall, that person was probably dead." Although he no longer deals in the black market, Hải still finds life in Germany trying because he cannot access welfare benefits. He works at a nail salon and sometimes goes from 9:00 a.m. to 6:00 p.m. without a break for food or cigarettes.

Hải always wanted to go to the United States, he recalls to the knowing nods of the others at that first dinner, because "the Vietnamese there are superior in skill, capacity, and intelligence compared to Vietnamese here." Clutching his hand to his chest, Hải says he must explain something to me, though it hurts him to say it: he does not associate with Vietnamese here because all they want to do is gossip and compare. He spends his time only with close family and friends, sitting around and eating just as we are doing now. The dinner continues in the same drab tone until Xuân suggests around midnight that we start heading home because I am lodging in the eastern neighborhood of Alt-Höhenschönhausen. Hải and Long immediately offer to accompany me to my tram stop. I decline several times, though I assure them that I am moving to a more central location soon. Relieved, they urge me to do so quickly, because "the communists" live there in the far east. On the way to the public transit stop, Xuân grumbles that Hải and Long have never offered to walk her anywhere. But they fussed over me, she supposes, because they associate my Vietnamese American background with morality and goodness.

On the one hand, Liên and Hải seem to shun structural explanations when it comes to the unequal ethnic nation. They see southerners as intrinsically more intelligent and capable. By contrast, they see northerners, including themselves, as living with compromised morality. In this logic, southerners' essential goodness grants them better lives, and northerners' essential badness dooms theirs. Liên and Hải did not consider this logic in reverse: that the contexts that received refugees in West Germany and the United States made it possible for them to survive or even thrive without legal or economic precarity.

On the other hand, both intuit what migration scholars have long asserted: the contexts under which border crossers exit their homeland have enduring repercussions. Hải recognizes how terribly his clandestine journey out of Vietnam and into Germany has constrained his life chances. Like the social workers introduced later in this chapter, Hải as well as Liên do not fault people for the stigmatized paths through which they left Vietnam. Instead, they blame the Vietnamese state for its failures to provide a livelihood for citizens in their homeland and for the "long arm of the state" that continues to make demands on them in the host country.[13]

Liên and Hải recognize that host country contexts shape the uneven resources with which border crossers can rebuild their lives, yet they blame not the German but the Vietnamese state for their meager opportunities. To Germany, they credit whatever gains they have been able to make. As a marriage migrant, for example, Liên enrolled in language classes that now enable her to comfortably navigate day-to-day life. Her language fluency translates to expanded job opportunities, although in practice this means she wakes up at 4:00 a.m. each day to prepare for her 6:00 a.m. shift, which leaves her plenty of time to pick up a second shift at home in the afternoons. Nevertheless, Liên sees the German language and integration classes she received as having enlarged her economic prospects.

By contrast, Hải talks about his membership in the Vietnamese nation-state as having condemned him to a demeaning and low-paying job. Arriving in Germany undocumented, Hải could not participate in the same integration classes available to his wife when she migrated earlier. As a result, he struggles to understand or respond to basic cues in German. More so than his wife, Hải's work visibly exacts a heavy toll on his well-being.

Indeed, the toll Hải's precarious work exacts on him becomes obvious when Xuân and I return to Liên and Hải's home for New Year's Eve. My partner, Will, accompanies us. The women shoo Will and me off to the living room while they finish cooking in the cramped kitchen. We try to make ourselves useful by entertaining Liên's toddler, who appears immediately fascinated by Will, who is White. "He loves Westerners," Liên and Xuân both remark matter-of-factly. Liên's toddler does indeed appear singularly transfixed on Will. This will soon ruin the peace of that New Year's Eve dinner. For now, Hải arrives home in low spirits. He greets me in Vietnamese, then shakes Will's hand and introduces himself in rudimentary German. Switching back to Vietnamese, he apologizes to me for being so late. He worked all day at the nail salon without food, he relays resignedly. To add insult to injury, he received a tip from only one customer, though he had five throughout the day.

Despite—or perhaps because—he seemed so defeated about his job, Hải arranges for me to join him at work three days later to "understand how average Vietnamese live and work in Germany." (Note here that Hải does not see former refugees as "average Vietnamese," because they presumably do not toil.) When I enter the nail salon at noon, two of Hải's coworkers have time only for the briefest of welcomes before customers start to trickle in. The cosmetologists spend much of the time in silence, punctuated by the occasional exchange between the owner of the nail salon and her German-speaking customers and snippets of conversation between the two female employees. Hải does not speak much with his coworkers and is unable to carry on conversations in German with his clients. The owner and three employees stay glued to their seats for the next several hours, quick restroom breaks aside. No one stops to eat. The shop officially closes at 4:00 p.m., but they all accept customers who arrived before the cutoff. They continue working by the time I head out at 5:00 p.m. for another engagement.

The symbolic ranking of the ethnic nation, with northerners on the bottom, applies even to people who have attained German residency or citizenship, like the nail salon owner. For example, self-employed northerners with residency also work protracted days that begin well before dawn. Their work stretches for weeks or months on end with few rest days. In part, this is a residue of former contract workers needing to show proof of income, among other requirements, to avoid deportation after the fall of the Berlin Wall.[14] Some turned to self-employment and opened convenience stores, food kiosks, and flower shops that have since become fixtures around subway stations. I sat for half a workday with a convenience store owner who subsisted on the occasional candy bar near her cash register. She had grown accustomed to the work and even managed to hire an employee so that her shift no longer ran from 8:00 a.m. to 10:00 p.m. Likewise, a wiry woman in her seventies ate and drank nothing during the hours I visited her flower shop. She had no one to cover for her were she to fall ill. Despite having permanent residency or citizenship in Germany, self-employed northerners nevertheless often experience a work tedium similar to that of Hải. These are certainly narratives of structural disadvantage, but what is key is that people interpret them as a result of belonging to the Vietnamese nation-state.

Northerners narrate their lives as part of a sweeping national experience in which grueling work consumes time and energy they would ideally dedicate to family. The combined stress of work and family come to a head after our New Year's Eve feast. Arriving home crestfallen from work and drinking himself into a stupor, Hải finally begins to relax. He taps away at his phone, completely absorbed in it, as his toddler jabs my partner with toys. Liên occasionally scolds her son, but to no avail. She apologizes to Will, then returns to the kitchen to wash dishes. I follow her and have just begun soaping when Will calls to me. Distressed, he walks into the kitchen with his glasses in his hands, broken in half at the frame. The toddler had whacked him in the face with a toy.

With the faucet still running, Liên rushes back into the room to chastise Hải: "What were you doing when your son broke someone's glasses?!" Hải wearily starts to offer apologies, his tiny peace snatched away. He tries to glue the frame back together, but his efforts are futile. Liên takes charge, insisting that they replace the glasses. Will and I tell her the glasses did not cost much, but she demands we meet at an optometrist's office that weekend. After some back and forth, we weakly acquiesce. Hải has slunk away during this verbal dance. As we prepare to ring in 2016, Liên sits next to me bemoaning her family life and how hard it is to live like this, all because she remarried a Vietnamese man. We are interrupted by a volley of fireworks going off all around us. The clock has struck midnight, and we rush downstairs to set off fireworks, Hải still conspicuously absent.

Days later when we meet at an optometry office, Liên and I have a private moment in which she laments her family troubles that stem, she intimates, from marrying a Vietnamese man who is a product of his national upbringing. She first shares that they are looking for a three-bedroom apartment. I ask if her toddler will stay in the same room as his teenage half-brother, but Liên scraps this idea. The teenager does not take care of his brother, she grumbles, even when she is busy in the kitchen and needs someone to watch her son for just ten minutes. Her husband is no different; he does not play with his young son either.

Liên speaks deliberately, as though we are sharing a secret, that "it is hard to be with a Vietnamese man after having been with a Westerner." She repeats that her first husband was so considerate. But when Hải comes home from work each day, he immediately gets on the phone. I utter some words of sympathy before Liên interjects, unprompted, that she cannot leave him despite their marital woes. Liên depicts her stepson as having no sense of responsibility, and she does not want her son to become spoiled because his parents divorced. And so, Liên ruminates, she remains committed—committed to living paycheck to paycheck in cramped quarters with an unhelpful husband, irresponsible stepson, and beloved toddler who nonetheless aggravates her already significant domestic load. Liên plainly resents these males in her life who operate according to what she sees as outdated Vietnamese standards. She came to question these standards, to expect better, during her first marriage to someone outside of her ethnic nation.

As we turn to next, social workers also devote much of their effort to addressing tensions within border-crossing families from the northern and central regions of Vietnam. The cases they arbitrate exclusively involve nonrefugee migrants. Hence, Vietnamese and Germans, laypeople and experts alike, converge on a shared understanding that individuals who experienced hardship at home in Vietnam heaved those hardships on their shoulders to Germany. There, such hardships manifest in irregular migration, work struggles, and familial tensions.

Social Problems as Northern Problems

Social workers and community organizers seek to remedy the challenges facing border crossers, focusing on people from the northern and central regions who, alone, seem affected by the poverty and politics of the Vietnamese state. The weekend before my first dinner with Liên and Hải, for example, I attended a Vietnamese Berlin Symposium that thematized these social problems. The event took place in the eastern neighborhood of Lichtenberg, where former contract workers as well as newly arriving migrants concentrate. A pamphlet advertised the event as "a forum for exchange between specialists from the respective subject areas and projects/associations of the Vietnamese community" (*ein Forum des Austausches zwischen Fachkräften aus dem jeweiligen Themenbereich und Projekten/Vereinen der vietnamesischen Community*). The forum, of course, includes neither former refugees nor refugee-founded associations.

Today's event is titled "The New Vietnamese Women: Opportunities and Challenges for Labor Market Integration" (*Die neuen Vietnamesinnen: Chancen und Herausforderungen für die Arbeitsmarktintegration*). "New" migrants include people such as Liên and Hải: "Lesser known is young Vietnamese who in the last several years have been coming to Germany through different paths, forming families, having children, and living in their own [ethnic] communities" (*Weniger bekannt sind hingegen junge Vietnamesen, die seit einigen Jahren über verschiedene Wege nach Deutschland kommen, Familien gründen, Kinder bekommen und zurückgezogen in ihren eigenen Communities leben*).

Like Liên and Hải, social workers rank the ethnic nation, putting northerners closest to the Vietnamese state and thereby the most deficient in terms of integration in Germany. Throughout the day, community organizers repeatedly specify that it is Vietnamese from the northern and central regions who warrant integration concerns.

Along with natives, the symposium features speakers and attendees with northern Vietnamese backgrounds, many of whom had left Vietnam decades earlier as contract workers. I had interviewed at least three of the audience members, all of whom worked for service organizations. Others I had heard of through casual conversations and secondary materials such as documentaries, pamphlets, and literature. The lineup and audience include people who played prominent roles in organizing for contract workers after the fall of the Berlin Wall. It included, for example, Ngọc Lan, the former contract worker-turned-social advocate who married an East German man before her contract expired (Chapter 3). Throughout the day's event, presenters focused on the harsh realities confronting former contract workers and more recent arrivals from the north-central regions of Vietnam. When speakers mention refugees, they do so by way of contrast with the lack of support that other Vietnamese border crossers received. The implication is that refugees do not confront difficulties or need social services.

We dive right into integration challenges with a lecture on "the new Vietnamese women in numbers" (*die neuen Vietnamesinnen in Zahlen*). An older Vietnamese man and a woman who appears multiracial, Asian and White, make the first presentation. They work for separate Berlin-based organizations that provide social services. Wearing a suit and speaking slightly accented German, the man begins a slideshow about the demographic profile of Vietnamese in Lichtenberg and neighboring Marzahn. Most people of Vietnamese descent living in the area, he notes, are Vietnamese citizens. He distinguishes three groups of Vietnamese border crossers in Germany: refugees from 1975 onward, who had free services (*kostenlose Leistungen*), contract workers, and asylum seekers today. The speaker lingers on this last group, emphasizing that "illegal [*sic*] Vietnamese live and work here," including "people who register outside of Berlin but live in Berlin" (*illegale Vietnamesen hier wohnen und arbeiten. . . . Leute, die außer Berlin anmelden, aber in Berlin wohnen*).[15] The female speaker, sporting a short haircut, dark pants, and a black trench coat, then takes her turn to discuss reliance on social welfare. Sixty percent of

Vietnamese women in this area, she explains, are "involved with social benefits" (*beschäftigt mit Sozialleistungen*).

The man resumes the discussion, describing the contingent refugees from the late 1970s and early 1980s as having "had everything . . . the contract workers [had] some [things], and the new Vietnamese [have] nothing" (*hatten alles . . . die Vertragsarbeiter teils, und die neuen Vietnamesen gar nichts*). He continues that asylum seekers now often travel through third countries such as Poland to get to Germany, their "motivation grounded in economics" (*Motivation öko gegründet*). New migrants face "difficult prerequisites" (*schwierige Voraussetzungen*), having often received incorrect information about their rights in Germany before they arrived. The audience, comprising social workers and concerned community members, raises further concerns during the Q&A session about illicit activities such as borrowing passports.

In a later presentation, speakers reveal that even some northerners who arrived nearly two decades ago have yet to fully settle. Three women lead this lecture about labor market activities, echoing the difficulties Liên and Hải confront. Working for the same prominent social organization in eastern Berlin, the presenters describe the services they provide to improve their clients' job opportunities. Prompted by an audience question, the speakers acknowledge that many of their older participants arrived in Germany as former contract workers.

Another presenter discusses tensions around raising youth, attributing family tensions partly to cultural practices and, more important, to Vietnamese parents' marginal positions in German society. (Again, "Vietnamese" cultural practices here do not seem to include those of former refugees. Their practices presumably are Germanized.) The speaker, a tall White man with a ponytail, specializes in youth crisis intervention and protective services. He recounts working with youth whose families have kicked them out for being LGBT, or children who fear their parents' reactions to their "bad grades—a 2," the German equivalent of a B. The speaker concludes with a somber overview: "Many Vietnamese don't speak enough German. . . . Most Vietnamese parents work six days a week . . . [and there is] a lack of information about their rights." (*Viele Vietnamesen sprechen nicht genug Deutsch. . . . die meisten vietnamesischen Eltern arbeiten sechs Tage in der Woche . . . [und es gibt] ein Mangel der Info über Recht.*)

Although the symposium presenters do not intend to cast blame, they do implicitly rank the ethnic nation. The experts in attendance mention refugees sparingly, and only then to make the point that refugees received full support and presumably face no difficulties that require intervention. The speakers neither fault people from the northern and central regions for their integration struggles nor praise southerners for their evident successes. Instead, they see border crossers' experiences as contingent on their contexts of exit from Vietnam and reception in Germany.

I had interviewed some of the social worker presenters and attendees of this event during previous fieldwork in 2014. In one-on-one conversations, they conveyed similar ideas around the legacy of their unequal ethnic nationhood—northerners, having felt the brunt of Vietnamese socialism, learned not to concern themselves with politics, which they see as emanating from the top down. Ironically, the same people who asserted this had also mobilized for residency rights in the 1990s (Chapter 3).[16] Importantly, these experts interpret the situations of northerners and nonrefugee border crossers in ways that affirm a key sociological principle: people are the product of their circumstances and history.

Social workers may not have moralized around these integration trends, but everyday Vietnamese border crossers certainly did. Northerners did so when they assessed their difficult lives as the inheritance of their national membership. Liên and Hải regularly disparaged the Vietnamese state and its citizens with negative stereotypes and proclamations. In the same breath, they praised southerners, many of whom fall outside the legal bounds of the sovereign Vietnamese state. The hardships Liên and Hải face owe to the contexts of their exit from Vietnam and the contexts of their reception in Germany. Yet they view their adversities strictly as evidence of how communism has corrupted Vietnam in general and northerners in particular, instead of, for example, a failure of the German state to protect all people within its territory. Liên and Hải offer some of the most searing criticisms of communism and the Vietnamese government, but most northerners I spoke with voiced similar ones. What is noteworthy is that everyday people articulate a relationship between region, history, and politics, reaching into the past for "historical events . . . [that] are reinterpreted to fit into a story that culminates in the politics of the present."[17]

Border crossers from different regions largely shared this politics of the present, criticizing what they saw as the corruption of the Vietnamese state and its inability to provide a livelihood for its people. Although this chapter centers on northerners' understandings of the ethnic nation and its attendant problems, southerners echoed these same refrains. They had done so since the fall of the Berlin Wall: recall that Kỳ, who came to West Germany through family reunification for refugees, rationalized to police officers in their small western village that the contract workers who were causing problems were victims of the collapse of communism (Chapter 3). Recent arrivals from southern Vietnam who did not leave as refugees also shared Liên and Hải's outlook. We spend more time with one of these post–Cold War southern migrants in the following chapter. What is important here is that Vietnamese people from across migration streams and regions of origin widely view northerners as victims of an authoritarian state.

Yet Cold War divisions remain salient precisely because Vietnamese see themselves and their coethnics as having been deeply socialized either under or in opposition to the communist Vietnamese state. Liên and Hải reason that they must marry for gain or break laws because their circumstances as members of an authoritarian country leave them with few options. And despite agreeing with them, many refugees with whom I spoke still believe that they could not overcome differences between themselves and coethnics who were socialized under the one-party system in Vietnam. The next chapter focuses on these fault lines, which southerners overwhelmingly police. In the meantime, our glimpses into Liên and Hải's lives and into the Vietnamese Berlin Symposium make clear at least one matter: northerners also recognize that their idea of the ethnic nation does not fully embrace southerners.

Though Liên and Hải wish that Vietnam had reunified under the South, they see southerners today as part of the ethnic nation but outside the nation-state. That is, Liên and Hải remain convinced of their shared ethnic nationhood with southerners but recognize that the political project of ethnic nationalism has failed. The couple may rue the Northern victory in Vietnam, but they neither imagine nor work toward the overthrow of the communist Vietnamese government. Instead, they have internalized the perceived failings of the Vietnamese state as their own. In their mental maps of the ethnic nation, Liên and Hải have propelled southerners and refugees off to greener pastures. Yet Liên and Hải do not assume that northerners fall outside the nation-state, even though the couple also live outside the territory of the home state and even as members of their family have German citizenship.

What defines belonging is not citizenship, but that Vietnam unified through the defeat of the South, which was absorbed into the political system of the North. Border crossers come to see the nation's social problems—postwar poverty, limited pathways to social mobility, and political discontent—as the problems of a northern region that then stretched across the territory of the reunified country.

Ranking the Plural Nation

Laypeople as well as experts interpret social problems as exclusively afflicting Vietnamese individuals from the north (and north-central) region. They therefore rank the Vietnamese nation hierarchically, southerners and refugees on top, (presumably northern) contract workers in the middle, and northern and north-central recent undocumented migrants on the bottom. The stereotypes that Vietnamese embrace about themselves do not come up solely or even primarily during private conversations. Rather, these stereotypes arise in the organizational contexts of everyday life, within families and at workplaces and community events.

Vietnamese border crossers subscribe to robust stereotypes about coethnics from different regions and, in their minds, corresponding migration streams. People largely reserved praise for southerners, whom they believed to be well integrated in Germany and other countries of resettlement.[18] This is evident, for example, when Liên states that southerners and refugees are "like natives" (*như người bản xứ*) in their language skills, education, and occupations. Southerners are law abiding, integrated, honest, and progressive—so the typecast goes. Because southerners represent the positive reference group, Vietnamese border crossers seldom felt the need to inform me about southern traits. Instead, people more often thematize negative stereotypes against those from the north. Border crossers from across regions described post–Cold War migrants from the north as law breaking, unassimilable, deceitful, and regressive. In previous decades, the media as well as refugees themselves attributed these same traits to contract workers.[19]

In one view, this might simply be a way for refugees, the more established group, to differentiate themselves from coethnic migrants and their attending stigmas. Mexican Americans in the United States, for example, at times emphasize their Americanness to distance themselves from Mexican immigrants.[20] They may do so to avoid hostility directed toward coethnics immigrants, going so far as to support restrictive immigration policies.[21]

But as this chapter has detailed, it was not only southerners or refugees who offered these negative portrayals of northerners. Liên, Hải, and our other dinner companions, Xuân and Long, recounted the law breaking they saw as being committed entirely by nonsoutherners—including themselves. And regardless of their backgrounds, Vietnamese border crossers explained these supposed regional differences in the same way: northerners' experiences under socialism in Vietnam impeded their chances of leading successful and moral lives.

Their logic is one of national belonging by taint. It is a logic we have encountered before. Recall that Phước, the son of a contract worker, described northerners as communist despite his own political convictions, and even despite his father's political disaffection after serving in the People's Army and conquering Saigon (Chapter 2). As a soldier, Phước's father saw himself as personally responsible for South Vietnam's defeat.

Liên and Hải, however, had not yet drawn their first breaths when the South fell. But though they disparage the Vietnamese state, they still unhesitatingly view themselves as part of its imagined family.

Extending the metaphor of family trees, Liên and Hải see refugees as having achieved purity through their exile, and subsequently as having transplanted their upright roots to better soil. By contrast, contract workers and, later, economic migrants contaminated their family trees by staying. They carry these with them to a land that is less hospitable to such corrupted roots. Liên and Hải did not extricate themselves from the trinity of citizen-state-territory even though they left the territory of their home state, and even though some members of their family have acquired German citizenship.

Border crossings therefore stretch the nexus of people, state, and place. State formation contributed to this in part because the fall of South Vietnam did not lead to the formation of a new state that melded North and South. Instead, South Vietnam was erased, and the North moved southward. This is perhaps one reason some who survived the war and still live in Vietnam today feel that they have been colonized.[22] In their thoughts and actions, Liên and Hải demonstrate how everyday people rank the ethnic nation after border crossings.

This differential belonging to Vietnam has continuing implications for how northerners and southerners relate to one another abroad. In their day-to-day lives, Liên and Hải rarely interact with southerners, many of whom share their political grievances. This is partly a legacy of their distinctive migration experiences, with refugees dispersing throughout the west and contract workers and more recent arrivals concentrating in the east. But as Chapter 5 explores, this also results from individuals and organizations working to enforce social divisions. And as we elaborate in Chapter 6, one group does so because they view the ethnic nation hierarchically and, like Liên and Hải, see southerners as its upper crust.

5 Choosing Friends and Picking Sides

ANH AND I FIRST MET at a holiday mixer hosted by Friendship and Adventure (FaA), the Vietnamese social organization comprising mostly northerners and former contract workers. Members gathered every two weeks in a building in eastern Berlin to practice cultural performances, host parties, and plan group travel. Unlike the other members, though, Anh does not hail from northern Vietnam. She also did not come to East Germany as a contract worker. A middle-aged woman from the Mekong Delta of southern Vietnam, Anh arrived in reunified Germany on a tourist visa in the early 1990s. At the time we met in 2015, she lived and worked in eastern Berlin, alternating her leisure time between FaA and Refugees for Germany (RfG), the Vietnamese social organization composed largely of southerners and former refugees who regularly meet in western Berlin. A vocal anticommunist, Anh's politics match those of RfG members I would come to know over the next several months. But despite her politics, and much to the ire of some RfG members, Anh indiscriminately befriends northerners as well as southerners, former contract worker and refugees alike. Unlike other RfG members, Anh does not hold the loss of South Vietnam against individual northerners.

I attend tonight's FaA mixer at the invitation of Hồng, Anh's sister, whom I had recently met at a Buddhist pagoda in western Berlin. Hồng had no particular interest in joining FaA, but she wanted to introduce me to her sister to help me recruit participants for my research. A first-time attendee of FaA's events, Hồng is accompanied by Kim (Chapter 1), an international student from central Vietnam who rents a room with Hồng. Kim had spent time in southern Vietnam while growing up, and she speaks with a southern accent. The number of Vietnamese speakers with southern accents at FaA's event swells with our attendance.

Nghĩa, a northern former contract worker, immediately takes note of our entourage, saying, "Saigon girls speak so sweetly" (*Con gái Sài Gòn nói chuyện ngọt ngào*). Southerners are kind, too, he adds. Nghĩa associates all of the south with Saigon, even though I am the only one who came from that city. Despite being renamed Ho Chi Minh City and stripped of its status as a national capital, Saigon remains the symbolic center of the south.

Recall that Nghĩa and his wife, Trinh, are former contract workers from the Eastern Bloc (Chapters 1 and 3). When the Berlin Wall fell, both filed for asylum in Germany and recollect being visited in their asylum camp by refugees. As others in the group would echo in the following months, Nghĩa expresses delight at having southerners attend FaA events. Like Liên and Hải from the preceding chapter, the northerners in FaA reasoned that people from their region had been influenced by communism, so they could not be fully honest or at ease. But southerners, they claimed, spoke like Germans: frankly. This sentiment would also come up publicly several months later, as FaA members prepared for a party to celebrate the group's anniversary. One of the men explained that the event was only for dues-paying members, but added that I was invited. "Do you know why? Because you're a child of the South," and therefore had been raised to be "comfortable" and "direct" rather than calculating.

Indeed, in my time with FaA and RfG over the course of the year, I rarely heard northerners say anything negative about southerners. Not a single northerner echoed DRV state rhetoric that southerners were American puppets. The reverse, however, was true: southerners routinely criticized northerners in ways that echoed the language of fallen South Vietnam. It might be the case that fallen nations have more pride, as with East Germans versus their compatriots in the West.[1] I suspect this also reflected my positionality as a southerner. Yet northerners readily criticized southerners who continue to wave the yellow flag and provoke tensions among coethnics. It was not, then, that northerners *never* criticized southerners, but that they criticized specific actions or individuals instead of attacking southernness. And they welcomed southerners into largely northern spaces, as with tonight's event.

The emcee soon announces the main entertainment event, karaoke, and the members shortly begin to clap along to "Spring over Ho Chi Minh City" (*Mùa Xuân trên Thành Phố Hồ Chí Minh*). Many of them still refer to the city as Saigon. Although the celebrations have just begun to pick up, Hồng declares at 5:30 p.m. that she and Kim are heading home. Accompanying them, I grab my coat and bid the attendees farewell, folding my arms and bowing my head to each elder. I trail behind Hồng as she hurriedly descends the stairs out of the building. Sighing, Hồng laments that she wanted to take me here to help me with my research, but she is leaving so abruptly because she cannot "play" (*chơi*) with northerners when all they want to do is sing this "red music" (*bản đỏ*). Neither Hồng nor her sister, Anh, came to Germany as contingent refugees. Nevertheless, Hồng claims that for "those of us who came here as refugees," these northerners stir hurtful memories of the theft of the South. Moreover, southerners would not come out here to the east to socialize, Hồng claims, because northerners are "hicks" (*quê*). Her depiction is telling because she repeated both before and after this event that she does not differentiate between north and south. She is happy to befriend anyone, she reiterates.

Hồng's abrupt departure from the FaA event exposes how friendship choices, which are not inherently national, nevertheless become national in their expression.[2] Like most other Vietnamese border crossers I met, Hồng spends her free time in the company of people from her region of origin. Yet unlike the northern couple Liên and

Hải (Chapter 4), many appear far less self-aware of how closed their social networks actually are. These networks often were quite closed, even though people often expressed an openness to befriending co-ethnics from different regions—or even when they deny being prejudiced, as Hồng does.

Why do these Cold War compatriots continue to choose friends and take sides based on northern or southern, contract worker or refugee allegiances? Vietnamese border crossers in Germany may not always intend to befriend only people from their same region of origin. Nevertheless, how different groups of migrants arrived in East and West Germany shaped their chances for encountering coethnics from different regions. Whereas refugees resettled in West Berlin, contract workers labored and lived in East Berlin and the Eastern Bloc more broadly. When Germany reunified, refugees had already established themselves in the western part of the city, and contract workers found their support systems among coworkers in the eastern part of the city (Chapter 3). In the decades since the fall of the Berlin Wall, however, Vietnamese have been free to move around the city. For their part, former refugees I spoke with have remained almost exclusively in the districts where they settled before 1989. Meanwhile, some former contract workers have crossed erstwhile borders by opening businesses in or relocating to the western part of the city. But decades after the fall of the Berlin Wall, friendship networks remain divided between north and south, contract worker and refugee, and legacies of communism versus anticommunism.

This chapter shows how social divides endure despite people's expressed welcoming intentions. It does so by connecting Vietnamese border crossers' cultural practices with group-level dynamics that regulate membership in social organizations. The following pages delve into these rigidly divided friendship networks by focusing on Anh, the southerner in FaA, and Hạnh, a northern international student in her early thirties. Each had her own motivations for joining FaA and RfG. An extrovert, Anh welcomed all opportunities to make new friends. Hạnh, quite reserved by comparison, needed survey respondents for a research study. Despite their different migration routes from Vietnam and regions of origin, both slotted into the northern organization, FaA, with relative ease. They would both run up against repeated gatekeeping by the southern organization, RfG. Neither woman perfectly fit the regional and migration combination of northern contract worker or southern refugee. As a result, their presence in both organizations illuminates conflicting understandings of the nation. They demonstrate how national symbols become commonplace, or banal, to some but charged, or hot, for others. Both women's ordeals reveal how the defeat of South Vietnam "instill[ed] a need to stage a return to the war's history again and again," here, through regulating friendship networks.[3] This helps us better understand how and why Communist-era social networks persist in postsocialist Berlin.

Northern Expressions of the Reunified Nation

Although Anh's critical position toward the Vietnamese government fits better with the political views of RfG, she actually gets along better with FaA than with RfG members. FaA members are also aware of Anh's political sentiments. She regularly shares posts about social ills in Vietnam on Facebook, even going so far as to tag FaA members in the posts to ensure that they see the critical articles. Perhaps surprisingly, then, Anh's politics do not seem to harm her relationships with friends in FaA. This might be because Anh is not the only one starting conversations about social problems in Vietnam.

Indeed, other FaA members write blogs and organize around social problems in Vietnam. One such person is Phong, an elderly man who arrived in Germany decades earlier as a contract worker. Some months into our acquaintance, Phong pulls me aside during a dance practice to urge me to study some of the most pressing matters facing coethnics of his generation in both Germany and Vietnam. Above all, he emphasizes the importance of medical information and access.

Although he is concerned with many of the same social problems as Anh, Phong focuses primarily on the quality of life of his compatriots rather than about how poorly he sees the communists governing the country. RfG members and southerners more broadly speak about the difficulties that former contract workers and new migrant arrivals from Vietnam face. But the locus of their concerns differs from that of northerners. For southerners, such discussions ultimately provide fodder for them to criticize the Vietnamese state, which many see as corrupt. For northerners such as Phong, these conversations center on the well being of a unified Vietnamese people. While Anh expresses dissent based on opposition to the Vietnamese state, Phong expresses dissent based on loyalty to the nation.[4]

Despite their shared denunciations of the Vietnamese government, southerners and northerners use language and symbols that reveal different levels of accommodation to the state's official discourse. This was true for younger Vietnamese, such as Hạnh and me, who were born after the war. Some months after I join FaA, I start to attend their events with Hạnh, a college student born in northern Vietnam in the early 1980s. For part-time work, she assists a researcher studying the mental health of Vietnamese in Germany. Hạnh needs to find respondents for a survey, and so she accompanies me to her first FaA meeting on Valentine's Day 2016. We sit quietly as FaA members discuss their upcoming events. Suddenly a woman, Sáu, barges in and begins to good-humoredly tease the men for not surprising the women with flowers today. Sáu explains that this day is about love and that friendship is a type of love. A skinny, bald man jokingly replies, "There are different kinds of love and we need to be clear [about what we mean]. There's romantic love or love for [former communist leader] Uncle Ho [Chi Minh]" (*yêu Bác Hồ*). Some attendees smirk, though most, including Hạnh, remain stone-faced. They appear evidently desensitized to this reference, which has sparked mass protests among Vietnamese diasporic communities abroad.[5]

Vietnamese people from different migration streams experience festivities through these uneven reactions to state discourse, so that a name or a flag that is simply national (cultural) to some is nationalist (political) to others.[6] On the day of the anniversary celebration we have been planning, FaA members arrive for setup at 1:30 in the afternoon. Anh's sister, Hồng, would not return to FaA during the remainder of my fieldwork. But her housemate, Kim, does. Another southern friend of Anh's, Mỹ Linh, also attends today. As the only young adults present, Kim and I serve desserts and take numerous group photos for FaA members. By 6:00 p.m., however, Kim is itching to go. I had told her earlier that I would leave with her. We gather our belongings and bid the elders farewell as songs continue to play in the background. Midway through one song, Anh runs up to Kim, Mỹ Linh, and me, and whispers indignantly: "It's red music!" (*Là bản đỏ đó*). Mỹ Linh nods disdainfully, decides she has tolerated the event long enough, and exits with us.

Mirroring my first time at FaA with Hồng, Mỹ Linh rages against northerners as we approach our bus stop. A southerner, she explains that she came to East Germany at a very young age as a contract worker. Mỹ Linh claims she did not know much about politics at the time. She did not differentiate between north and south during her youth, she explains, as she met few northerners in her southern hometown. But she learned about the politics of north and south on German soil. In particular, Mỹ Linh became socialized into the southern refugee stance of mistrusting northerners after the fall of the Berlin Wall. Despite her contract worker background and willingness to share the same physical space with northerners, Mỹ Linh's mistrust of northerners leads her to openly disparage them.

The concerns of northerners such as Phong, as well as the experiences of southerners such as Anh and Mỹ Linh, highlight how people from opposite regions of Vietnam experienced reunification asymmetrically. Vietnamese reunification under the direction of the North means that these symbols have become a form of "banal nationalism" for northerners.[7] As the North's vision of a reunified Vietnam actualized, its accompanying changes became taken for granted, including the renaming of Saigon as Ho Chi Minh City. Yet the mention of Hồ Chí Minh reminds southerners of what they see as the occupation of the South. Anh and Mỹ Linh take offense at a city name to which the northerners in the room had become accustomed. To those who lament the outcome of reunification, the same symbols represent objects of hot nationalism.[8] This reveals how national symbols and the messages they convey "are mixed because symbols . . . mean different

things to different people at different times."[9] People who were border-
crossed unevenly by the reunification of Vietnam, hence, come to experience national symbols unevenly.

But although they accept these symbols, northerners like Phong
do not necessarily support the actions of the reunified Vietnamese
government toward its citizens. Rather, they see the state as an imperfect but nevertheless legitimate representation of their nation. Phong
is an avid newspaper reader who has many connections with journalists writing about social problems both in Vietnam and among Vietnamese communities abroad. His singing along to "Spring over Ho
Chi Minh City" during an earlier FaA event did not signal unwaver-
ing support for communism, though Anh and Mỹ Linh might read his
behavior in that way.

Toàn, another FaA member, goes even further by suggesting that
unlike northerners, southerners are pure because they are not tainted
by communism in the way that he suggests he and other northerners
are. But unlike Liên and Hải, the northern couple from Chapter 4,
Toàn does not grumble that Vietnam would be better off today had
the South won. He simply does not concern himself with this coun-
terfactual because the war is over. Like Phong, Toàn can happily sing
along to songs about Ho Chi Minh City as a depoliticized, literal reference to a place in southern Vietnam. Although both men harbor criticisms of life under communism, they concern themselves less with
formal politics and more with what the political fact of reunification
means for everyday people. By contrast, southerners like Anh fixate
on what this means for the legitimacy of the state.

In the midst of these competing understandings of the nation,
FaA continues to welcome even ardent anticommunist southerners
such as Anh. The event space itself remains, on the surface, depoliticized because of its established, albeit implicit, northern identity. Yet
northerners in FaA at times call attention to southerners' "allergies"
(dị ứng) to reminders of communism, such as the flag of Vietnam.
War and conquest hence inform the experiences of not only refugees
but also of their nonrefugee coethnics, and, ultimately, of how these
two groups relate to one another.[10] A northern former contract worker

summed it up with a phrase: "We have to give the losers something to live with." By this, he meant that northerners simply had to accept the hatred of southerners.

Although northerners at times acknowledge the contested nature of their homeland's history, the triumph of the North means that they also have the privilege of going about their lives without much thought to the grievances of those who lost the war. The symbols and references the northerners in FaA circulated show that "signs of nationalism can be too familiar to be noticed," having become banal.[11] But what northerners perceive as banal nationalism, southerners instantly regard as signs of hot nationalism.

Southern Commemorations of the Nation in Exile

After their nation-state collapsed, Southern nationalists organized cultural events around their experiences of war, nostalgia, and suffering. These "ecstatic" events celebrate "a particular national community on a mass public scale with reference to symbols and assumptions that inform an understanding of everyday life in a world of nations."[12] Unlike FaA, RfG members directly involve their children in their activities. RfG serves as the only place where the second generation can learn the Southern version of the war, history, and nation.[13] RfG organizers remind their children of the first generation's loss through cultural performances such as mournful songs. By contrast, the northerners and former contract workers in FaA host events purely for enjoyment. FaA members do not often bring their children to meetings, and they sing songs that they see as Vietnamese, not northern. Because southerners and northerners experienced the outcome of their nationalist struggle in different ways, northerners can sing along to "Spring over Ho Chi Minh City" without feeling that they are committing an overtly political act. For those who lost their capital of Saigon, however, the northern naming of people, places, and things reminds them of defeat and longing.

Outsiders can readily detect this "refugee nationalism" as well.[14] For example, Hạnh's introduction to this exile identity came in winter

2016 shortly before the Lunar New Year, the most important Vietnamese holiday. After leaving an RfG planning meeting, I head to a nearby church to attend an event advertised as a cultural night and Lunar New Year Celebration of the Year of the Monkey (*Đêm Văn Nghệ Vui Xuân Bính Thân*), hosted by the Vietnamese Refugee Community of Berlin (*Cộng Đồng Người Việt Tỵ Nạn Berlin*). I arrive just after 6:00 p.m. and locate Hạnh, who has been waiting in the auditorium where performances will soon take place. Children as young as four perform "yellow songs" (*nhạc vàng*) that invoke life in pre-1975 South Vietnam. Midway through one of the performances, Hạnh uneasily points out the sign above the stage, which reads "Freedom Spring" (*Xuân Tự Do*) and is etched onto the pattern of the yellow-striped flag of former South Vietnam.

While the night's carefully choreographed performances and display of national symbols "united [southerners] in the transitory awareness of heighted national cohesion,"[15] these same cues signaled national division to others such as Hạnh. I grew up in the United States, where the imagery of the yellow flag is common. I am therefore unfazed by these Southern symbols—that is, until I notice Hạnh shifting uncomfortably. The realization dawns on me just as Hạnh comments that she is not accustomed to seeing this flag. Her reaction reveals a discrepancy between how border crossers from different regions experience the red and the yellow flags. Because Vietnam reunified under the direction of the North, the red flag with a yellow star hangs today and officially signifies the country to the international community. By contrast, the yellow-striped flag represents a nation-state that no longer exists on the world map. It cannot therefore become banal in the same way.

As we leave some hours later and walk over to the light rail station together, Hạnh confides that she felt disconnected (*abgetrennt*) in the southern setting.[16] People kept their distance, she believes, and she suspects that they perhaps did not want to get to know her. Hạnh shares that before I arrived at the event, she was trying to recruit an older southern woman for the survey. The woman declined but observed, "I hear communists are all rude and disobedient. But you're not."

I initially laugh at the assumption that, based on Hạnh's northern accent, she must be communist. But then I recall my recent interviews with RfG members, some of whom have openly stated that they do not trust northerners. In particular, I think back to a conversation with Chính, a southern refugee and one of RfG's core organizers, who explained it this way:

> For me, there's a feeling of insecurity [when I encounter northerners]. . . . Insecure in that when we associate, there's a sense of distance, we can't be completely honest with one another. So that's how I feel toward friends who are northerners, and I tell them as much. They also understand. They also understand. They say they understand, [they say,] "I get you," . . . because northerners are used to living with the communist regime, so they rarely speak the truth. . . . But southerners are like Germans: [they're] direct.
>
> (*Đối với chú thì có cái cảm giác là không có an toàn. . . . Không an toàn là khi chơi mình có một cái khoảng cách, mình không có thật tình với nhau được. Thì cái đó là cái mà chú cảm giác đối với bạn bè người bắc chú cũng nói vậy. Họ cũng hiểu. Họ cũng hiểu. Họ nói hiểu, [nói] "tôi hiểu ông" . . . tại vì người bắc họ sống quen với chế độ cộng sản, ít khi nào họ nói thật. . . . Thì cái người nam thì giống như người Đức: thẳng.*)

Chính's words reinforce the Cold War Berlin–Saigon analogy, a framework of seeing Cold War frontiers in different locales as being intimately connected. As then US National Security Advisor Mc-George Bundy explained in 1965, "[T]he defense of Berlin, right now, is in Vietnam."[17] Chính and other refugees deploy this rhetoric to link themselves to the struggles of West Germany and how it emerged victorious over East Germany. Chính's words further reveal his conviction that people can be trusted only to a limited extent after living under a communist system. I heard these beliefs echoed from multiple respondents, both northerners and southerners.

With Chính's words resounding in my mind, I cannot think of a way to assuage Hạnh's concerns about trying to connect with southerners for her survey. Before we arrive at our stop, I tell her I hope our elders will not apply these regional divides to the younger generation who did not live through the war. Hạnh replies, despondently, that she feels that they do anyway. She steels herself for the possibility that she might again feel excluded at the RfG event taking place in a week's time. But she feels the pressure to meet her quota of southern respondents because her deadline looms.

As Hạnh anticipates, the RfG Lunar New Year celebration would involve just as many symbols of refugee nationalism and just as many missed connections for recruiting survey respondents. On the day of the celebration, RfG members arrive at City Hall at noon to begin preparations. After unloading decorations and other supplies, the women and girls immediately change into *aó dài*, traditional, fitted silk tunics with flowing pants.[18] While men could wear suits, the women, including me, had to wear the áo dài. The outfit served "not just [as] a vehicle for expressing Vietnamese femininity, but a pedagogical tool for inculcating it."[19]

Indeed, much of the planning for today's event revolved around showcasing South Vietnamese practices to German audiences and, in the process, bonding the two together in national unity. The festivities take place in a rectangular hall seating two hundred Vietnamese and White attendees, ranging from the elderly to teenagers and very young children. Two flags hang down from the ceiling, bordering the left and right sides of the stage: the red, black, and gold flag of the Federal Republic of Germany and the red-striped bear flag of Berlin. Two smaller flags also decorate the stage at eye level: a second German flag and the yellow-striped flag of former South Vietnam.

The event officially begins at 5:00 p.m. with "Call to Citizens" (*Tiếng Gọi Công Dân*), the national anthem of the obsolete Republic of Vietnam, blaring over the speakers. Having been relieved of my duties registering people, I enter the hall just as the borough mayor, a White woman, wraps up her introductory remarks. She draws a parallel between the successful integration of Vietnamese refugees decades ago and her hopes for the welcome and resettlement of Syrian refugees now. After the borough mayor's speech, roughly a dozen

RfG members gather at the front to sing "A New Year Toast" (*Ly Rượu Mừng*). The chorus proceeded:

A a a a
Let us fill our glasses
Wish everyone well
A a a a
That hearts be full of charm for life

. . .

Somewhere far away there is an old mother
Longing for her son's return, her sight blurred by the tears
Wishing her a homeland soon
(With) her son returning in loving reunion.

(*Á a a à*
Nhấp chén đầy vơi
Chúc người người vui
Á a a à
Muôn lòng xao xuyến duyên đời

. . .

Kìa nơi xa xa có bà mẹ già
Từ lâu mong con mắt vương lệ nhòa
Chúc bà một sớm quê hương
Đứa con về hòa nỗi yêu thương.)

I mouth along with the words, having grown up with both the South Vietnamese anthem and New Year's toast. Like many others present, I did not simply witness this southern national bond but, rather, produced it "through the collective act of performance."[20] Hạnh signals with a shake of her head that she does not recognize the song. She cannot jointly produce this version of a south Vietnamese national bond.

Hạnh experienced both refugee events, the cultural night and Lunar New Year celebrations, as jarring. Symbols of refugee nationalism contrasted sharply with her experiences of growing up in northern Vietnam and socializing with her northern relatives and their social circles in eastern Berlin. The aunts and uncles in RfG, as we addressed them, at times made earnest efforts to include Hạnh in conversations, even if only to patronizingly lecture her about the blunders of communism. Yet to Hạnh, they retained an emotional distance that she found palpable and unsettling. Feeling pessimistic about her prospects of soliciting survey respondents when she felt so out of place, Hạnh heads home from the festivities shortly after arriving.

Friendship networks thus remain homogeneous because of both self-selection and social pressure from others, both often facilitated by competing nationalist symbols. The southerners in RfG actively choose to spend time around coethnics from their region of origin, who ostensibly remain loyal to the same defunct flag. Newcomers trying to gain entry would run up against this in-group mentality. Had Hạnh not needed southern respondents so urgently, she would not have been eager to enter a space that proved so uncomfortable. Although no one told her she was unwelcome in the space, Hạnh nonetheless gathered this from the built environment full of Southern symbols and from the cues she read from others. She experienced symbols of refugee nationalism as stifling because the "assumptions of nationhood and the dominance of the national 'imaginary' have not just produced exclusive communities but they have, in effect, blocked out alternative ways of imagining the political past and present."[21] Of course, southerners like Anh at times experience northern spaces similarly. But because the North won the war, that scenario perhaps appears more unavoidable—natural, even.

Toeing the Anticommunist Line

The anticommunist tenor of RfG is so evident that even long-time members feel they need to tread carefully. This was true for Loan, an elderly RfG member who dreads confrontation around controversial issues. We have just paused for dinner after the Lunar New Year performances and relocated to an adjacent hall, where a bonanza of dishes has been laid out. As I look around for a seat, Loan beckons me to her. Born in the north before the division of Vietnam, Loan migrated southward. She later married a Southern soldier and arrived in Germany through family reunification for refugees. Loan insists on talking to me today because she will be taking an extended trip soon. Amid the commotion in the dining hall, she explains in hushed tones that she will be visiting Vietnam through early summer and does not want other RfG members to find out.

Loan paints a climate of political intolerance toward return travel, one that is lent credibility by the fact that some RfG members spurn travel to Vietnam. These boycotters see spending money in Vietnam, even for a few days or weeks, as directly contributing to an authoritarian regime. At least two of the RfG core members have not been back since they departed in the 1980s. The first is Chau, who came to West Germany through family reunification for refugees. She sees return travel as a direct form of support for the Vietnamese government and stated on several occasions that she would never return unless the red flag were toppled and the yellow flag reinstated. Chau scorns return travel out of a deep rejection of the Vietnamese state:

> So many of my friends go back to Vietnam. So I ask, when you fled by boat, you were afraid they'd catch you, right? So now why do you have to go back to Vietnam? You go back to Vietnam firstly, OK, you say you go to visit family, visit your parents. But when you fled, did you ever think there'd be a day when you'd return to visit your parents? No. But now they've opened their doors. . . . We go back and bring money to the country of Vietnam, but who are we nurturing? We can't nurture our people.

> (*Bao nhiêu người bạn của cô đi về Việt Nam. Cô mới hỏi, lúc mày đi vượt biên, mày sợ nó bắt lại chứ gì? Bây giờ tại sao mày phải về Việt Nam? Mày về Việt Nam thứ nhất OK, mày nói mày về thăm gia đình, về thăm cha mẹ. Nhưng lúc đi vượt biên có bao giờ mình nghĩ có một ngày mình trở về mình thăm cha mẹ không? Không. Nhưng mà bây giờ nó mở cửa ra. . . . Mình về là mình đem tiền về cho xứ Việt Nam mà nuôi ai? Không phải nuôi được người dân của mình.*)

Through gritted teeth, Chau maintained that bringing money to Vietnam created greed among the citizenry, because return migrants cannot possibly help everybody in poverty. Instead, returnees rouse in those who live in Vietnam a vision of what they could have become had they been able to leave.[22] This money from abroad corrupts, Chau insisted, leading people to steal and degrade themselves to satisfy their greed. Her resolve gave way to sobs at this point as we sat eating ice cream at a mall food court. She wept that she would love to see "our Vietnam" again, so full of natural beauty. But she would never do so until the communist regime collapsed. Because Chau considers return travel "no different from giving money right to those old men [communists]" (*chẳng khác nào đưa tiền vào cho các ông nội đó*), she also resents Buddhist nuns who travel to Vietnam (Chapter 6).

Hòa, a second RfG member who shuns return travel, is more militaristic in his homeland politics. Unlike Chau, who migrated through family reunification, Hòa escaped by boat. A former officer in the South Vietnamese army, Hòa was imprisoned in a reeducation camp after 1975. He fled Vietnam in the early 1980s, resettled in West Germany, and by 2016 had not returned to Vietnam in more than thirty-five years. Unlike Chau, however, Hòa does not speculate about the conditions under which he would return to Vietnam. The matter is settled: Vietnam is communist, and Hòa has no desire to be part of that nation-state.

But Chau and Hòa do not privately avoid return travel to Vietnam; they also share their unsolicited opinions with others. Hòa did so on first meeting Hạnh. She had been attending RfG events with me for nearly three months when she met Hòa. He approached us to spread the word that he had a spare room for a student to rent. Once a year, he added—signaling his politics—he allows protesters to stay at his home. I asked him what they protested against and he replied, "the communist regime" (*chế độ cộng sản*). He insisted that "because Hạnh is a northerner," he had to make it clear that he was opposed to the regime rather than to individual communists.

It is in this context of open anticommunist rhetoric in RfG that Loan tells me about her travel plans in whispers. Even if RfG members do not directly chastise people for visiting Vietnam, the anti-regime attitudes of some of the more vocal members alert the rest to which themes might be better left undiscussed in that space. To avoid real or imagined reprimand for visiting Vietnam, Loan conceals her plans.

Loan takes special care to hide her travel plans to Vietnam during a festivity that invokes "ecstatic" rather than banal nationalism.[23] Celebrations such as the cultural night and Lunar New Year liberally deploy symbols of Southern and refugee nationalism and nostalgia. Regional insiders and outsiders alike readily detect these undertones. Vietnamese who are neither southerner nor refugee, or just one but not the other, do attend. But they come despite potential discomfort caused by political icons. For example, some northern former contract workers who attend pagodas in the eastern part of the city also participate in refugee celebrations. If they have qualms about the yellow flag as Hạnh does, they know to be discreet about it because of the southern dominance over the space. Thus, people who attend refugee events feel compelled to adhere to certain norms around mentioning return travel and to avoid discussing certain political topics. That is, they feel pressure to talk, choose, perform, and consume the nation in particular ways.[24]

Red-Baiting Northerners and Their Allies

Some southerners did not simply hint at or demonstrate an anticommunist affect; they also actively censured individuals whom they considered politically suspect. During my fieldwork, Hòa provided the most striking example. On a spring afternoon in 2016, I meet Hòa at the subway station near his apartment to interview him. We talk about the neighborhood as we walk up to his one-bedroom apartment. He furnishes his living room, which he rents out, with two sets of bunk beds set against opposite walls of the room. A mantle stands in between the bunk beds, paying homage to leading South Vietnamese political and military figures. Guerrilla warfare patterns hang all over the walls, along with the South Vietnamese flag and posters of protests against Vietnam. Hòa proudly points me to a poster he made as part of a larger tribute to five Vietnamese generals who committed suicide on April 30, 1975, instead of cooperating with Northern forces. Military insignia hang below the poster. (See Figure 5.1.)

Hòa proudly furnishes photos of himself from when he escaped Vietnam as well as pictures of the groups of people he stayed with in a camp in the Philippines. When I remark on how young Hòa looked in photos with his military garb, he produces the uniform as well as badges from the division in which he fought.

Hòa is genial enough with me but adopts an entirely different tone with it comes to Anh, whom he clearly considers a traitor to the Southern cause. After our interview, Hòa asks about my plans for the day. I reply that I plan to visit Anh at her workplace. Hòa decides he will accompany me because he is friends with Anh's boss, but he does not hesitate to tell me that I am a bad judge of character because Anh is not someone I should trust. He continues to lecture me as we leave the apartment, claiming that Anh has a habit of exaggerating (*nổ*) and that he does not trust her propensity to start new business ventures and then run them into the ground. By disparaging Anh's entrepreneurial tendencies, Hòa equates her experiences with those of (northern) contract workers after the fall of the Berlin Wall, some of whom engaged in various black market activities in order to make a living (Chapter 3).[25]

For her part, Anh appears oblivious to Hòa's frostiness—though, as an outspoken anticommunist, why would she think that he considers her politically compromised? When we arrive at the restaurant where Anh works, she greets us with a wide smile. Hòa claims that he and I ran into each other at the subway station. Not realizing that I had just interviewed him, Anh pleads with Hòa to help me with my research. He grumbles that he will invite me over one day but that he welcomes into his home only those who are willing to protest communism—implying that she is not. Although Hòa had mentioned upcoming protests to me, he does not invite Anh or assume she would even be interested. His comment aimed to chastise Anh for her seeming lack of allegiance to refugee nationalism, a sentiment he assumes I hold because my father had been imprisoned like him. But Anh is busily restocking and does not linger on his words.

Figure 5.1 Hòa's mantle commemorating the fallen Southern nation, May 2016. Source: Author.

The already tense situation worsens after another man in his sixties enters the restaurant. Lộc is the husband of the owner of the restaurant. We briefly introduce ourselves to each other before Anh suggests that while they are both there, Lộc and Hòa can fill out a brief survey. She hands each a copy of the questionnaire Hạnh is distributing for part-time work. Lộc flips through the survey and immediately claims that it was sent by communists. He and Hòa cite as their evidence that the survey asks for their names, dates of birth, addresses, and a host of questions about their religion and other details that they consider intrusive.

As Anh and I exchange troubled looks, I interject to say that the researchers offer an honorarium to participants and therefore need personal information to prove to funding sources that real people participated in the study. Lộc responds aggressively that only communists would ask these questions. Anh joins in to deescalate, saying that a student is distributing this survey and Anh is just helping her out of goodwill. Addressing Hòa, I add that I have asked him similar questions about religion and politics, and he did not think I was a communist. He reacts sharply that I do not ask people to write down their answers—though, I wonder to myself, *Is it really any better that I voice-record them and take photos of their homes?* Recognizing that I need to defuse the situation, however, I do not say this out loud.

The two men egg each other on, Hòa saying he will take a copy and scribble, "Pay me 30,000 [euros] and I'll fill this out." Anh intervenes authoritatively here, saying that Hòa can take a survey only if he intends to fill it out. This hostile back-and-forth continues for well over an hour, as customers come through to order items for takeout. Lộc and Hòa have gulped three beers each when Anh says to Hòa that when he invites me over for an interview, he should invite her as well. Hòa responds flatly that she is not invited to his home. Good-naturedly, Anh says that he and Lộc are both invited to her upcoming birthday party. Dismissing her gesture of friendliness, Hòa mutters that he is not interested. Lộc abruptly complains about the survey again, spitting out chunks of roasted peanut that he has been snacking on with his beers.

I try to explain that I know Hạnh, the student passing out the survey, and that she really is just a student assisting in research to earn some extra income, not a communist spy. Hòa has met her as well, I remind him. He did not hesitate to talk to her about his political beliefs face-to-face. For comparison, I emphasize that I ask many of the same questions in my interviews. At this mention, Hòa snaps that I can ask him anything because I am from the United States and, more important, am the child of a Southern officer who was imprisoned by the Communist regime. Had I been from (northern) Vietnam and asking him these questions, he would have "strangled" (*bóp cổ*) me. Anh scoffs at his comment, but Hòa insists he is not joking. His stare, tone, and composure indicate complete seriousness.

Despite his pugnacity, Hòa largely spares me his spite, as though I am politically inoculated by virtue of my father's long captivity. Instead, he directs it all at Anh. At around 6:00 p.m., I prepare to head out, and Hòa decides to leave with me. Anh excitedly remembers that she has found me someone to interview and suggests that we meet with that person next week. I thank and hug her before I leave. Not two steps out of the door, Hòa begins to berate me for being so naive. He accuses Anh of helping me, as she is helping Hạnh, for instrumental reasons. I defend Anh, saying she just wants to support students who are in Germany without our usual support networks. Hòa ignores me. Instead, he contemplates making a copy of the survey and forwarding it to the leadership of RfG to demand that they deny Hạnh access. Although frustrated, I recognize that proper decorum here demands I not rebuke my elder. I tell Hòa instead that the lead investigator of the study has already been in touch with RfG. He insists that that does not matter. He will confront the leadership and if, for example, one person votes to allow Hạnh to distribute the survey but another does not, Hòa will know who is a communist. I stop engaging. Hòa ignores my nonresponse and moves on to other topics before he exits the subway at his stop.

Gatekeeping and Forcing Allegiances

Despite her congeniality toward everyone, Anh had increasingly become troubled by RfG members' antagonism toward her over her choice to befriend northerners. The day before her birthday party in spring, I arrive at her home to help with preparations. I relay to Anh that Chính from RfG asked me to invite her to an event later that evening. On hearing what I just said, Anh glares disbelievingly.

Although Anh introduced me to RfG and had known the aunts and uncles longer than I did, she no longer communicates with them much. Nor does she receive direct invitations to RfG events. Anh complains that Chính's wife, Mỹ Yến, claimed that they could not attend her birthday party because of a conflict with Buddhist events taking place in Berlin and Hanover on the same day. Anh assumes that the couple lied because the two pagodas coordinate to avoid conflicts. When Anh informed Mỹ Yến about her rescheduled birthday party, Mỹ Yến replied curtly that they were busy. On Anh's birthday, Mỹ Yến did not call or text to wish Anh well. Because of this, Anh exclaims, she is done with RfG and tells me not to bring them up again.

For their part, RfG members do not seem to wonder why Anh has stopped showing up at events. An hour after leaving Anh's, I arrive at the RfG event in the farthest eastern fringes of what used to be West Berlin. Since April, the organization has been meeting at this location to barbecue outdoors and enjoy the good weather. Vũ, one of the organizers, greets me and then remarks that I am arriving so late in the day. I explain that I was with Anh earlier. He quietly goes back to barbecuing. His wife, Vy, then asks how Anh's birthday party went, but I clarify that it is not until tomorrow. She also says nothing more. Neither would attend the party the next day. I then go inside to greet each elder before coming back outside to sit on a bench and enjoy the evening.

Even Mỹ Linh, Anh's friend who occasionally attends FaA events to support her, does not seem to take notice of Anh's long absence from RfG. As we eat, Mỹ Linh starts to talk to Kiều, the international student we met earlier who became a refugee in West Germany after South Vietnam fell (Chapter 2). A core RfG member with northern roots, Kiều nevertheless chats with Mỹ Linh about how northerners always add some type of herb to their food that "we" do not. They say other things about northerners before Mỹ Linh mutters, seemingly embarrassed, that a northerner is sitting right next to them. Appearing to be in her sixties and sporting a pixie haircut, the woman is busy on her phone. Mỹ Linh explains in a low voice that the woman recently received political asylum in Germany, having been a dissident in Vietnam. Although the implicit regional membership of RfG is southern, the organization welcomes northerners who have demonstrably rejected communism by protesting or fleeing.

Mỹ Linh then introduces me to Kiều's husband, who straightaway interrogates me about my political background by asking about the place I call home. I respond "the United States," and he notes, apparently satisfied with my accent and answer, "So [you're one of] our people, not one of [the communists'] spawn" (người mình, chứ không phải con ông cháu cha). After making polite conversation, I go inside to catch up with Tài, a staunchly anticommunist refugee who was born in the north but migrated to the south when Vietnam divided in 1954 (Chapters 1 and 2). He coyly asks if I spend a lot of time "over there" (*bên kia*) for my research. Tài repeats this without actually specifying that he means the east. Notably, the building we are in today is quite far east, though it belonged to West Berlin before German reunification. Tài is clearly referring to a political rather than a simply geographic location. I confirm that I do go "over there" as well. Chau, the RfG member who boycotts travel to Vietnam, then interjects to catch up with me before we begin to clean up and head out together.

On our walk to the subway, Chau asks about Hạnh, not having seen her attending RfG events for some time. I explain that Hạnh has a separate engagement today but will likely attend next time. I then relay to Chau how, when Hạnh accompanied me to the cultural night, a stranger said she thought all communists were rude but that Hạnh did not seem rude. As I recount the story, I laugh at the audacity of the woman's comment. Chau, however, responds matter-of-factly: "It depends on what the education in the family was like" (*Cũng tùy theo giáo dục trong gia đình như thế nào*). She does not consider for even a moment that Hạnh might not be communist. In this us-versus-them mentality, Hạnh and other northerners are communist until proven innocent, as with the northerner who recently claimed asylum in Germany.

Friendships in the Shadow of a Fallen State

Hạnh's difficulty gaining the trust of RfG members, and their eventual ostracization of Anh, make clear the impact of border crossings on people's everyday lives. Hạnh intuitively anticipated and then repeatedly encountered southerners' mistrust of her, which she—and they—attributed to her northern background. Anh's experience exposes another dimension of the complex friendship networks in postsocialist Berlin: even though Anh is a proud southerner and anticommunist, she too encounters gatekeeping by RfG because of her choice to befriend northerners.

The women's decisions to engage with both FaA and RfG run up against forces that push them toward one organization over the other. For FaA members, their acceptance of Vietnamese reunification under a one-party communist system manifests in their use of names, phrases, and songs that invoke official state discourse that has become banal. This turns off southerners such as Anh's sister, Hồng, who never returned to FaA after her first visit. Or Mỹ Linh, who occasionally comes to FaA at Anh's behest but does so only while ridiculing the northerners around her. FaA membership remains mostly northern, but southerners' nonparticipation is voluntary. For their part, the leaders and members of FaA do not police membership and instead welcome anyone who wants to socialize.

Southerners thus choose not to engage with northerners, their objections to certain words and references demonstrating that the banality of national symbols is a social achievement. It is an imperfect achievement at that, because individuals experience symbols differently along a continuum of banal to hot nationalism. RfG, by contrast, reserved access for those it deemed properly aligned with refugee nationalism. People in the organization repeatedly reject Anh's attempts at friendship once they realized that she befriends both northerners and southerners. They also refuse to fulfill Hạnh's requests that members participate in her survey.

Regional divisions endure because both groups demand adherence to the underlying regional, migratory, and accompanying national(ist) identity of a social space. FaA demands this implicitly by honoring certain historical figures and holidays. RfG demands this explicitly by questioning the allegiances of even self-identified anticommunists. Yet members of both groups largely share criticisms of the Vietnamese one-party state. As is the case with Liên and Hải in Chapter 4, shared politics do not overcome social networks that are regionally bounded. The exceptions are northern migrants to the South such as Kiều and Tài or recent border crossers who take on very real risks when they oppose the Vietnamese government. What happens, then, when border crossers from different regions of origin and with different relationships to the Vietnamese state have to share physical space? We turn to this in Chapter 6, which examines the only social institution where people from both migration streams and regions of origin regularly come together.

6

Buddhist Meditations in Northern and Southern Accents

MY SEARCH FOR AN INSTITUTION where northerners and southerners, former contract workers and refugees come together brought me to Linh Thứu Buddhist Pagoda in summer 2014. The property appears empty on my first visit there, with only one older Vietnamese man silently watering the lawn. I wander past him to the back of the building and peer into a spacious kitchen. A middle-aged man and woman greet me, imploring me in northern accents to keep my shoes on as I start to untie my laces before entering the religious space. I introduce myself as a student researcher trying to volunteer here. The woman suggests I speak to the abbess for permission. But first, they insist I have some lunch. Neither says much as they take turns serving me fruit and a vegetarian vermicelli soup. After I finish eating, the woman directs me to the cellar downstairs to speak to the nuns.

The quiet of the two northern disciples cooking and cleaning upstairs contrasts with the commotion downstairs, where five nuns and six disciples cram around metal tables in makeshift assembly lines. The nuns wear gray robes; one elderly man, three older women, and two teenage girls wear jeans and T-shirts. They spread out across three tables, working together to make desserts. The team at one table rolls out dough, another wraps dough around a vegetarian filling to form balls, and a third covers the dough balls with plastic and loads them onto trays. Mistaking me for someone else, a woman asks, "Why didn't you come on Sunday" (*Tại sao không đến chủ nhật*)? I explain that I have just come for the first time to the pagoda. "From where" (*Từ ở đâu*)? "From the United States," I say. Appearing satisfied, she ushers me into the production line, where I transfer the balls of dough to a table for the elderly man to line them into trays. As I move between tables, different people take turns asking, "Where are you from in the United States" (*Ở đâu ở Mỹ*)? "How long are you here" (*Ở đây bao lâu*)?

In the haste and uncertainty of this first encounter, I miss that all of them—nuns and lay disciples alike—speak with southern accents. I realize this only as a woman at a table farther away begins to sing "Saigon Is Beautiful" (*Sài Gòn Đẹp Lắm*) and then jokingly adds, "Saigon girls are beautiful" (*Con gái Sài Gòn đẹp*). Another playfully responds, "It's girls from My Tho [another city in southern Vietnam] who are beautiful" (*Con gái Mỹ Tho mới là đẹp*). The elderly man, Tín, begins to ask me questions about my background. As Tín would later describe, he escaped Vietnam by boat after his wife bore their first child. They feared the implications of the three-generation life history for their newborn (Chapter 2). By the time we meet, Tín has been in Germany for more than three decades: "I escaped by boat in 1981. You hadn't been born yet" (*Bác vượt biên năm 1981. Lúc đó con chưa sinh ra*), he correctly deduces.

As discussed in earlier chapters, border crossings reconfigure the nexus of people, state, and territory in enduring ways. Everyday people actively reproduce the identities created by border crossings, such as southerner and refugee. They also police membership in these groups, as we saw through Anh's and Hạnh's struggles to access to Refugees for Germany (Chapter 5). By the time I completed my fieldwork in 2016, Linh Thứu Pagoda remained the only social institution that regularly brought Vietnamese worshippers from different migration streams and regions of origin together. (This has to do in part with the pagoda's founding, which we delve into shortly.)

How, then, do everyday Vietnamese border crossers navigate a religious site that tries to erase regional and political identities or, at the very least, asks disciples to leave them at the door? Religious sites like Linh Thứu can be great unifiers in the lives of international migrants, playing a bridging role between them and the host society.[1] Migrant religious institutions can help newcomers ease into their environments, develop civic skills, and pass on cultural traditions to the next generation.[2] Religion can also be a source of strain between migrants and host societies, as well as among migrants from the same origin country.[3] We see this, for example, in tensions between Indian American Hindus and Muslims over meanings of "Indianness."[4] The lay believers who come to Linh Thứu, however, do not compete over which religion represents their Vietnameseness. Instead, they share a commitment to Buddhism, and many consider it synonymous with their ethnic identity.

Linh Thứu Pagoda thus offers a unique vantage point into the relationship of religious practice, border-crossing communities, and homeland politics because the contestations there occur among people who share religious, ethnic, and national identities. Recall that the northern couple, Liên and Hải, see their ethnic nation as an "imagined family," albeit one segmented by degrees of belonging to the homeland and host country (Chapter 4). In most aspects of their lives, however, Liên and Hải do not encounter their estranged ethnic kin. This is decidedly not the case for lay disciples at Linh Thứu Pagoda. Their weekly gatherings at the pagoda are more like awkward family reunions. This often takes on some form reflecting my first day there: northerners and southerners physically divided even while on the same pagoda grounds. To be clear, "Buddhism is not a neutral, transcendent belief system, but historically a major player in Vietnamese politics."[5] The lay disciples whose stories fill these pages, however, stressed Buddhism's otherworldliness. This chapter therefore explores how disciples negotiate coethnic divisions in a shared religious space that they see as emphasizing harmony.

Southern "Lifelong" Buddhists versus Northern "Rememberers"

Refugees founded Linh Thứu Pagoda during the Cold War, which set the tone for how they would come to see Buddhism as both a spiritual and political haven. Refugees imbued their house of worship with their experiences of exile as they resettled in West Berlin, an island of capitalism surrounded by the socialist East German state. In the 1980s, they established a small study group, Linh Thứu Buddhist Mindfulness Road (LTBMR; *Niệm Phật Đường Linh Thứu*) as part of a broader faith network in West Germany. For major holidays, refugees and their families had to travel to Viên Giác, a larger, more established pagoda in the West German state of Lower Saxony. To reach Hanover from West Berlin, they needed to cross through East Germany to get to the rest of West Germany. One disciple of LTBMR who referenced these journeys was Lan (Preface). She arrived in West Berlin in the 1980s through family reunification for refugees and recalled,

> It wasn't just my feeling, but was the feeling of many people at the time, feeling very uncomfortable. And a sense of insecurity because back then when I came here I was still very afraid of police. And especially of police of East Germany because they're police of a Communist country. . . . Their faces were very cold.
>
> *(Không phải là cảm giác riêng của chị, mà lúc đó là cảm giác của rất nhiều người, cảm thấy là rất là khó chịu. Và một cái nỗi bất an vì mình lúc đó mình qua đây là mình vẫn còn rất là sợ cái chuyện công an. Mà nhất là công an của Đông Đức tại cái đó là công an của một nước cộng sản mà cái khuôn mặt họ rất lạnh lùng.)*

Lan's characterization of the border agents as cold matches how native West Germans experienced crossing through East Germany as well. This was exactly what the East German police wanted. Former East German police, for example, referred to their own postures, glares, and attitudes before 1989 as a "fuck-off position" meant to intimidate civilians.[6] These actions affirmed for those in the West that the socialist state in the East treated people inhumanely.

Despite encountering threatening East German officers, refugee disciples continued to make trips into the East out of commitment to a religion that they had grown up with and that they had brought with them across borders. None of the refugees who spoke with me identified as converts who found Buddhism while abroad. Instead, they were people whose families had practiced Buddhism in Vietnam and saw themselves as lifelong believers. It was therefore imperative for these disciples to cross the East German border several times a year to reach Viên Giác Pagoda. These trials affirmed refugees' commitment to their religion as well as to their exile identity. In this historic context, refugees saw Buddhist houses of worship as a safe haven in a heartless, communist world that threatened to encroach on them.[7]

After the fall of the Berlin Wall, refugee disciples welcomed contract workers into their religious space with ambivalence. Southern disciples of the fledgling pagoda, such as Thắm, whom we met earlier, offered assistance to people they saw as their ethnic kin (Chapter 3). But though their subjective understandings of a shared identity ran deep, it did not correspond to a closely knit community.[8] Thắm, for example, began to view contract workers negatively when she observed the women flirting with her husband. For their part, many former contract workers had heard of LTBMR's outreach efforts through the nuns, pagoda publications, and hearsay. Some original LTBMR members still lived in Berlin in 2016, but many of the contract workers they had helped had moved to newer pagodas in the city or other cities in Germany.[9] Some had repatriated to Vietnam. But even so, refugees were no longer in the majority, as the pagoda membership grew and the physical space relocated and expanded over the course of the 1990s.

Despite this demographic shift, contract workers and northerners who later joined the pagoda still felt that Linh Thứu belonged to refugees because of the Cold War context in which those refugees had founded the space. New arrivals perceived that the pagoda still privileged the experiences and, by extension, the presence of southerners. Đẹp was one such northern disciple who felt dismayed when she began to attend the pagoda in the early 2000s. Arriving in Berlin shortly after German reunification, Đẹp "knew that pagoda belonged to the southerners." These "readings of space" reveal people's subjective interpretations about which group's experiences are privileged and, hence, who claims ownership over the pagoda.[10]

Like southerners, later northern arrivals to the pagoda also drew on historic conditions in Vietnam to explain differences in individual religious practices and understandings. Northerners often made claims to the same effect as southerners that circumstances in their home region prevented northerners from exercising their faith. This was true for Đẹp, who sharply contrasted the pagoda in Berlin with how she experienced religion in Vietnam:

> In the north, religion is not like it is in the central region or in Saigon. . . . [In the north] you go to pagoda and you beseech [Buddha]. You plead for yourself and for your family. . . . [But I later realized you go to pagoda] to change your life and your way of thinking, to be blissful.

> (*Ở ngoài bắc thì phật giáo nó không có như trong miền trung hoặc trong Sài Gòn . . . em lên chùa thì em cầu xin . . . xin cho bản thân mình và cho gia đình thôi . . . để thay đổi cuộc sống của mình và cái suy nghĩ của mình để nó hạnh phúc.*)

Đẹp recalled being a young woman in northern Vietnam and going to pagodas to pray for success in finding a husband. Chuckling, she added that young people still do this today. Rather than attributing this to youth or lack of insight into religious teachings, Đẹp saw it as an issue of the northern region not understanding Buddhism. It was not until Đẹp began attending pagoda in western Berlin, surrounded by southern nuns and disciples, that she felt she had a breakthrough in understanding the teachings of Buddhism.[11]

Like Đẹp, Cúc had to contend with religion's lack of immediate relevance to her everyday life in socialist Vietnam. A northern former contract worker who faithfully attended a pagoda in the eastern part of Berlin, Cúc explained that she did not seek out Buddhism back in North Vietnam because she was a young adult with a busy work schedule who "did not know to go to pagoda" (*cô cũng không biết đến chùa*). Moreover, "in the North, there were very few pagodas in the rural areas, and they didn't have monastics" (*Ở ngoài miền bắc chùa vùng nhà quê thì ít, không có sư*). Visitors who came to be on sacred grounds could therefore not even benefit from teachings by spiritual leaders.

More generally, northerners and southerners alike viewed the ability to exercise religion in the North versus the South as having shaped the regions' divergent relationships to "authentic" Buddhism. Shortly after the Democratic Republic of Vietnam came to power in 1945, it began to curtail the rights of religious communities.[12] This made visits to pagodas in the North very risky, as Huệ, the cadre who feared xenophobic violence after the fall of the Berlin Wall, relayed (Chapter 3). As a young adult in North and later reunified Vietnam, Huệ visited pagoda twice a month, on the first and fifteenth of the lunar calendar. Fearful of being exposed, she had to sneak off (đi lén) during lunch breaks to hide her pagoda visits from others. Huệ recalled an atmosphere of immense religious intolerance at the time as the government demolished pagodas. This trend continued after Vietnamese reunification, when the state declared religious gatherings to be criminal.

Whereas southern disciples had been at least nominally Buddhist before migration, several northerners "became active Buddhists only after migration in a (post)socialist context."[13] People who lived in North Vietnam met obstacles in pursuing their religion because of the country's doctrinal atheism, which complicated the practice and transmission of their faith. The northerners who began attending pagodas in postsocialist Germany were not converts per se, but instead simply had not practiced Buddhism even though it may have been in their families before the DRV assumed power.[14] But because of this disconnect in northerners' religious practice, southern disciples at times characterized northerners as out of touch with proper Buddhism.

Yet devout northerners and southerners expressed identical understandings of Buddhism, emphasizing that people should come to the pagoda to learn to lead a moral life rather than to pray for blessings. However, Huệ would eventually boycott the western pagoda following nationalist confrontations discussed shortly. She would self-study at home for years until the founding of the eastern pagodas. Đẹp, the northerner who felt that Linh Thứu belonged to southerners, committed to coming to the house of worship to liberate her mind from material concerns and to focus on improving herself spiritually. Huệ and Cúc, both northern former contract workers, attended their pagoda in eastern Berlin nearly daily. During their visits, they cleared weeds, replaced incense in and mopped the prayer halls, chanted meditations, and generally carried the burden of maintaining the property. They and other (often female) former contract workers committed themselves to their pagodas with more intensity than many former refugees I met. Nonetheless, in the eyes of some southerners, this perceived difference between northern "rememberers" versus southern "lifelong" practitioners undermined northerners' claims to Buddhism.

When Nationalism and Religion Collide

Religion and nationalism need not be at odds. Even before 1954, essays and periodicals revealed how "the Buddhist faith was thus not just compatible with nationalism; it also compelled the faithful to defend their nation."[15] But in post–Cold War Berlin, religion clashed with competing nationalisms at Linh Thứu. As contract workers began to attend the pagoda in larger numbers, refugees reasserted Linh Thứu's alignment with Southern, refugee nationalism. They achieved this most viscerally through using political symbols such as the flag of fallen South Vietnam. Some refugee disciples carried the "Freedom and Heritage Flag" with them into the pagoda, stitched onto their clothes, tucked into their bags, sticking out of their pant pockets. They consumed the nation in hypervisible ways.[16]

Sơn, a northern contract worker who attended one of the pagodas in eastern Berlin, reasoned that refugees brought these flags to the pagoda to provoke people, create discomfort, and stake claims:

> You go to pagoda and carry the flag of the Southern regime back then. . . . Then northerners come to pagoda over there so the two sides look at each other uncomfortably. . . . [They bring the flag to say] "This pagoda is ours, not yours."

(Ông đi chùa thì ông cầm cờ của chế độ miền nam ngày xưa. . . . họ đem
theo đến chùa. Rồi người ở bắc đi sang bên chùa bên đấy thì hai cái phía
nhìn nhau có vẻ khó chịu. . . . "Cái này là chùa của bọn tao chứ không
phải là chùa của chúng mày.")

Sơn derided the flag wavers at Linh Thứu as uncultured (*thiếu văn*
hóa) because educated people would never do such a thing. Yet he did
not criticize the yellow flag out of allegiance to the communist government, which had executed his landowning grandparents (Chapter
2). Sơn similarly disapproved of other reminders of the war, such as
old army uniforms. For him, the national division that resulted in two
flags had long been resolved. Hence, he saw reminders of that division
as deliberate needling.

Seeing refugees' flag waving as a provocation, some former contract workers deserted the fledgling Linh Thứu Pagoda, never to return. Huệ, one such person, explained:

> [The people at the pagoda in] Spandau . . . opposed communism. [I]
> went once and they hung the yellow stick flag [a derogatory term for
> the South Vietnamese flag]. Here [we're] revolutionaries so we don't
> go anymore [to Spandau] . . . Because they hang that flag and under-
> mine our revolution.
>
> *(Spandau . . . chống cộng. Đi một lần họ treo cờ ba que. Đây cách mạng*
> *thì các cô không đi nữa. Không đi nữa . . . Không đi đó về sau. Tại vì nó*
> *treo cờ nó chống phá cách mạng mình đó.)*

Huệ turned her back on the western pagoda even though she urgently
needed community. After the fall of the Berlin Wall, she lost her job,
experienced xenophobic attacks, and feared that she could be deported at any moment. Despite her vulnerability and potential benefit
from the social networks at the western pagoda, she was turned off
enough by refugee nationalism that she renounced the only Buddhist
community available to her.

It was not the case that Huệ objected to displaying *any* flag at the
religious site, however. To Huệ, the red flag of present Vietnam would
have been most appropriate and "prettiest," as it represents Hồ Chí

Minh, who in her eyes had made reunification possible. Indeed, pagodas founded by Vietnamese contract workers in the former Eastern Bloc contain state-legitimizing symbols, so the tension is rooted not in mixing religion and politics but in bringing the wrong politics into a religious space. Buddhist teachings and pagodas have thus "become a major site of contesting people's relation to Vietnam."[17]

By the time I arrived at Linh Thứu, decades after these nationalist confrontations, southern and refugee disciples largely remained silent about the developments that resulted in national flags being discouraged from the pagoda. Indeed, it was former contract workers who recalled that the nuns intervened in political affairs, reminding their disciples to focus on the teachings of Buddhism to detach from this-worldly affairs. They dwelled not on the specifics of the nuns' efforts but on the results: by reminding disciples of the teachings of their faith, the nuns encouraged these coreligionists to reconcile their antagonisms. Đẹp, the northern disciple who initially felt that Linh Thứu Pagoda belonged to southerners, noted what she saw as a positive change in the dynamics at pagoda:

> I think that later the Buddhists [disciples] made more . . . bigger [events], like expanding [the pagoda]. . . . Then at that time northerners came a lot, too. . . . Then after a time the Buddhists who had been coming to pagoda for a long time [southerners and refugees], I think, also understood the words of the scriptures so people no longer rushed into a temper like in the early days anymore.

> (*Chắc chị nghĩ sau này thì phật tử cái chùa mới làm nhiều . . . lớn hơn, kiểu như rộng rãi hơn. . . . Thì khi đó thì những cái người bắc thì người ta cũng đến nhiều . . . Dần một thời gian các phật tử mà đã đi chùa lâu chị nghĩ chắc là cũng hiểu những cái lời nói của kinh thì người ta không còn những cái sân si như cái ngày thời mới đầu nữa.*)

When I asked refugee disciples about the flag controversy, they, like Đẹp, stressed that true believers heeded the nuns' teaching to put aside their nationalism in the religious space. Anticommunist flag wavers either modified their behaviors or left the pagoda.

But even if the nuns' intervention successfully calmed nationalist divisions, some coethnics still experience the pagoda as belonging more to southerners than to northerners. Southern expressions
of Vietnameseness continue to set the tone for how lay disciples consume and perform the nation. This was apparent on the Penultimate
Lunar New Year's Eve in early 2016, a holiday that revolves around
family. Vietnamese households customarily prepare feasts on this day
so that the spirits of deceased ancestors may descend to share a meal
with their loved ones. The offerings include plates of fruits and candies that people have laid out on the prayer hall floor. The nuns take
turns reading off a list of names of deceased family members, relayed
to them by lay disciples who make an accompanying monetary donation to the pagoda. Downstairs, volunteers have rearranged the dining
hall into tight rows of circular tables set with vegetables, pastries, and
a hot pot for cooking broth. To the right of the stage at the front of the
hall, yellow apricot blossoms, commonly found in southern Vietnam,
branch out from an ornate vase. Northern Vietnamese tend to use
pink cherry blossoms instead. A succession of karaoke singers takes
turns on the stage as visitors to the pagoda feast.

In between live performances, prerecorded music plays in the
background, including repeats of "Cry a River" which begins:

I often think of home in the afternoons
Especially on rainy afternoons
Luckily, Cali rains seldom
Unlike Saigon
Otherwise, I'd have cried a river.

(Tôi hay nhớ về quê nhà vào buổi chiều
Nhất là những buổi chiều mưa rơi
Cũng may Cali trời mưa ít không như Saigon
Nếu không tôi đã khóc một dòng sông.)

The lyrics recall the loss of the South Vietnam with its capital in Saigon. Reinforcing this exile status is the reference to California, the
state with the largest concentration of Vietnamese outside Vietnam

and considered the economic, cultural, and political "capital of Viet-namese in exile."[18] Turning to me midway through the chorus, Hồng, from southern Vietnam, points out that all the songs are from the south—implying to whom the pagoda belongs.

Beyond the actions of individual anticommunist disciples, Linh Thứu continues to reflect southern claims on the space through its built environment. For example, a poster that hung on the walls of the pagoda throughout winter 2016 advertised an upcoming event for the "Vietnamese refugee community of Berlin" (Chapter 5). Linh Thứu also maintains exchanges and continues to coordinate events with Viên Giác Pagoda, which identifies itself as a refugee religious community. The pagoda publishes a regular magazine that features the South Vietnamese flag on the cover. One of the most durable features of the built environment suggesting a southern bias is a black sign hanging on the wall of Linh Thứu, linking the pagoda with the Unified Buddhist Sangha of Vietnam (UBSV).[19]

The UBSV formed during the religious conflicts of the 1960s in South Vietnam. Buddhists alleged that then President Ngô Đình Diệm, a Catholic, discriminated against their religion in favor of his own.[20] On the eve of celebrations of the Buddha's birthday in May 1963, Diệm banned the display of religious flags. Only days earlier, however, the Vatican flag had flown at a government-sponsored event in honor of Ngô Đình Thục, leading cleric and Diệm's brother.[21] In an ironic and fateful twist, Diệm "seems to have imposed the flag embargo mainly because he was annoyed with the overzealous character of the commemoration for Thuc."[22] Subsequently Buddhists took to the streets in mass demonstrations. A month later, the monk Thích Quang Đức self-immolated in protest of the treatment of Buddhists. Following the 1963 religious crisis, monastics formed the UBSV. After 1975, the government of reunified Vietnam treated the UBSV as a threat. The black sign hanging on the front exterior of the pagoda therefore squarely aligns Linh Thứu with an organization considered illegitimate by the current government of Vietnam.[23] (See Figure 6.1.)

The built environment of the pagoda is not static, however. In recent years, former contract workers who became successful entrepreneurs

Figure 6.1 Linh Thứu Pagoda, January 2016. Source: Author.

have contributed large sums of money to the pagoda, allowing the nuns to construct an elaborate, two-story building in western Berlin. Accompanying symbols of northern belonging have also crept into the built environment. One example comes from a small pillar to the right of the front entrance, clearly recalling One Pillar Pagoda, one of Vietnam's most iconic structures in the current capital of Hanoi. The built environment thus reflects ongoing contestations over ownership of and belonging to Linh Thứu. Hence, national controversies become mapped onto architecture. (See Figure 6.2.)

In the Name of Buddhism

Because national flags are discouraged at the pagoda and the built environment is in flux, disciples have resorted to contesting coethnics' religiosity rather than their politics. As with boundary making in friendship networks, it is largely southerners who make these distinctions between their understanding of Buddhism versus that of their

Figure 6.2 Linh Thứu Pagoda's pillar, August 2014. Source: Author.

northern coethnics. One key example comes from Chau, the Refugees for Germany member who boycotted return travel to Vietnam (Chapter 5). A southerner who came to West Berlin in the 1980s through family reunification for refugees, Chau was a lifelong Buddhist who had attended pagoda while growing up in South Vietnam. Contrasting those experiences with how she interpreted northerners behaving at pagoda, Chau described them asking for blessings for their businesses. While conceding that northerners truly believed in Buddhism, Chau felt that they had a limited understanding of the faith:

> The northern brothers and sisters over there, their [faith in] Buddhism is real but they don't understand [Buddhism]. They just make offerings. They think there are spirits or something. They go into pagoda, they say, "Teacher, can you make an offering for me for fortune in my business?" . . . Do you know what the nuns say? "OK, let me do it." That means the nuns don't know what Buddhism is. Our Buddha says not to worship spirits. We have to understand the religion. . . . What kind of pagoda makes offerings for people in their business? . . . I don't think it's right.

*(Mấy anh chị người bắc ở bên kia, đạo phật là đạo thiệt nhưng họ không
có hiểu. Họ cứ cúng quải. Họ tưởng như thần linh vậy đó. Họ vào chùa, họ
nói "cô ơi, cô cúng giùm cho con để con làm ăn được may mắn." . . . Biết
sư cô nói gì? "Được rồi, để cô làm." Vậy là sư cô đâu có biết đạo phật là gì
đâu. Phật mình nói là không cúng vái thần linh. Mình phải hiểu đạo. . . .
Chùa gì mà đi cúng cho người ta làm ăn? . . . Cô thấy không có đúng.)*

Chau further implicated the leadership in corrupting the religious
space. She candidly portrayed the nuns as ignorant, divorced from the
tenets of Buddhism, and led astray by money:

Back then when I went to [the fledgling] pagoda, it still seemed like
a pagoda. You could meet with the abbess, nuns, they would come
to talk to disciples. But then the pagoda expanded . . . then they expanded some more, then I started to dislike it. I am a Buddhist. Our
pure Buddhism says we shouldn't show off that way. Now we come
to make offerings, there's no closeness [of the nuns] to disciples, [the
nuns] don't lecture for disciples to understand the religion. Whoever
offers a lot [of money], the nuns will come down [from their quarters
upstairs] to greet them. Whoever offers little [money], forget it.

*(Lúc đó cô đến chùa cô thấy nó còn có cái vẻ là chùa [when it was still
LTBMR]. Gặp được ni cô, sư cô, đến nói chuyện với đệ tử. Còn sau khi
mở chùa lớn . . . lại thêm chùa lớn nữa, thì bắt đầu cô lại không thích.
Cô là người đạo phật. Cái đạo phật thuần tuý của mình đó là nói mình
không có nên phô trương theo cái kiểu đó. Bây giờ vào cúng quải, gần
gũi đệ tử không có nè, giảng cho đệ tử hiểu đạo giáo không có nè. Ai
cúng nhiều thì sư cô xuống chào hỏi. Ai cúng ít thì forget it.)*

Chau alleged that the infusion of contract workers to the western pagoda, and their focus on the material, had upended the values of the
leadership. Beyond worship practices and whom the nuns seemingly
favored, she also expressed concerns about proper behavioral codes.
She balked at the pagoda blaring karaoke over the speakers, which she
considered an abuse of sacred space. Her criticisms were consistent
with her lack of regard for the nuns and her view that they were not
representatives of a true Buddhist path.

Chau's complaints about northerners' and the nuns' alleged behaviors at pagoda reflect a gendered framing of religious practices.[24] For example, a study of Buddhist Canadians finds that women tended to make offerings and carry out rituals and that the few men present studied texts and exuded the air of the educated, in touch with core beliefs. Chau's comments reproduce this gendered hierarchy, modified with the figure of the feminized, ignorant northerner versus the educated, devout southerner who stayed true to the faith. Yet Chau did not mention the flag wavers or the pressure on nuns to intercede to maintain the peace at pagoda. She also largely limited her criticisms to the realm of the religious. In other situations, Chau has made abundantly clear how much the yellow flag means to her (Chapter 5). It is therefore all the more noteworthy that Chau frames her complaints about northerners and nuns at the western pagoda in chiefly religious rather than nationalistic language. Following these religious convictions, Chau had long since abandoned the pagoda. Her actions parallel those of lay Buddhists in Ho Chi Minh City today who distrust and "actively reject monastic authority and completely sidestep institutional hierarchies."[25]

The ways history and homeland connections matter thus extend beyond the political, making the sphere of the religious a battleground for coethnic factionalisms. Like Chau, other lay disciples mapped coethnic divisions onto old configurations of North and South, but couched them largely in terms of the religious instead of the political. They did not frame the nuns' involvement in coethnic reconciliation as political, though the spiritual leaders are surely the subject of intense competing partisan pressures. But disciples did not simply mask political grievances through religious frames. Instead, the presence of contract workers and refugees in a shared pagoda space meant that religion, in addition to shared ethnicity and nationhood, became a discursive site of negotiation. Nationalist politics did not disappear; instead, people drew on shared religion as a frame for expressing difference and mapped these logics of difference onto labels of north and south, contract worker and refugee.

Although Chau left Linh Thứu, the disciples who remained needed to reconcile the tensions they felt between the teachings of their faith and how they interacted with coethnics from different regions of origin. Like other southern disciples committed to the pagoda, Hồng (from Chapter 5) knew that being prejudiced against northerners fundamentally went against how she understood Buddhism.[26] Nevertheless, she used to bristle at seeing northerners at the pagoda when she began attending in the early 2000s. She assumed northerners were all "godless atheists" (*vô thần vô thánh*). "Back then, people hated hearing the language [accents] of northerners" (*Trước đây, nghe tiếng người bắc là người ta ghét*), she declared. After the dust settled from the flag-waving trial, southern disciples such as Hồng knew they ought not to alienate northerners with their Southern nationalism.

Instead, Hồng's grievances revolved around the higher moral authority she supposedly occupied because of her relationship to truer Buddhism. Hồng readily shared her view of northerners' "ludicrous" (*buồn cười*) religious practices—even to northern acquaintances she was meeting for the first time. She did so when we met at Linh Thứu in autumn 2015. I had been speaking with Xuân, a recently arrived international student from northern Vietnam whom I met several weeks earlier and who would later introduce me to Liên (Chapter 4). Seeing me give my business card to Xuân, Hồng starts to ask about my studies. Assuming I am a student from southern Vietnam, Hồng's interest piques when she learns of my American background. She insists I sit down and chat with her. Xuân joins me, and Hồng introduces us to Kim, a newly arrived student who is renting a room with her (Chapters 1 and 5).

Hồng promptly invites us back to her home, where she tells us about how she had tried to support smaller, poorer pagodas in the eastern part of the city that are largely attended by northerners. She stopped attending, however, because "northerners always have drama." Hồng adds, though, that she has friends who were northerners as well as southerners (but recall her stern reaction to the northerners in Friendship and Adventure from Chapter 5). Many of Hồng's southern friends stopped attending Linh Thứu when northerners began to arrive in large numbers.

As Xuân, Kim, and I continue eating fruit, Hồng gets down on her knees to mimic what she saw as northerners' absurd actions at the pagoda. She enacted, for example, how northerners would carry with them into the prayer hall a large, showy gift basket full of fruits, candies, and cash arranged out so that people could see the extent of their generosity. Rather than parting with the donation before entering the prayer hall, Hồng claimed, northerners would sit jealously with it right next to them, to signal to everyone exactly whose contribution and magnanimity it was. Rather than making the poised, mindful movements of bowing and kneeling, they would feverishly shake their palms as though possessed, Hồng caricatured. After all that, northerners would then leave just one part of the offering, for instance, an apple. She alleged that the northerners would then haul the rest of the loot home with them. Hồng chuckles at the silliness of these actions, which to her indicate an ignorance of proper behavior in a sacred space. Again, Hồng had no qualms about reciting these stereotypes about northerners in front of Xuân, who is from the northern port city of Hai Phong.

Although Hồng still takes the opportunity to mock northerners' actions in the sacred space, she maintains that she gradually learned to tolerate their unusual behaviors at the pagoda. She credits this change of heart to her husband, Hoàng, who implored her not to judge northerners too harshly for their ignorance. They were plagued by famine and poverty in the North, he reasoned, and so had become used to begging Buddha for material blessings when they attended pagoda. Hoàng concluded that Hồng should not blame northerners for their backward customs (*phong tục*). By contrast, he saw southerners as having had enough to eat and as being prosperous because of the fertile Mekong Delta in the south, so they could develop a higher understanding of Buddhism.

The undertone of Hoàng and Hồng's rationalization is that poverty and suffering left northerners unable to conduct themselves in a civil manner—quietly, humbly, and graciously in the way they assume southerners do. Even while seemingly absolving northerners of blame, Hồng and Hoàng treat them as inevitable by-products of socialization under communism. In this way, the southern couple resemble northerners Liên and Hải, who correspondingly see themselves as fundamentally corrupted by the communist state.[27] Hồng and Hoàng also repeat the tropes of southern lifelong Buddhists versus northern "rememberers" or converts, a dichotomy present since the first contract worker began to attend the pagoda.

In the name of Buddhism, Hồng sought a tenuous peace in a religious space that for the foreseeable future would include both sides of the estranged imagined family. The southerners who could not tolerate the presence of northerners, however, rarely gave that as the reason they exited. Like Chau, they instead claimed that northerners' contributions to the pagoda corrupted the nuns, who allowed the infusion of money and material desires into the sacred space. Also in the name of Buddhism, people such as Chau would abandon the pagoda. Only disciples who were willing to leave their overt nationalisms at the door remained at the pagoda.

A Tenuous Peace

Amid this fragile peace, disciples at Linh Thứu Pagoda continue to self-segregate within their house of worship. This was as apparent during my first visit to Linh Thứu in summer 2014 as when I returned for fieldwork in fall 2015. Arriving at 10:00 a.m. on a Sunday, I plant myself in the kitchen to help with lunch preparations as dozens of disciples chant in the prayer hall upstairs. The three other volunteers in the kitchen are elderly northerners, one man and two women. One of the nuns sets me and the women to work peeling taro, a starchy root with fuzzy skin. Struggling to grip the taro with kitchen gloves on, I remove mine. Within minutes, my hands redden and begin to itch terribly. One of the women scolds me, saying that at my age, I should have had enough experiences with cooking to know this was going to happen.[28] She instructs me to wash my hands with salt for the itchiness and sends me off to rest. In the dining hall, I sit down at a mostly empty table across from a young woman with short hair who appears to be in her thirties. Watching me claw my hands, she meets my eyes,

smiles, and entreats me in a southern accent not to scratch. Turning
to her mother, who has just sat down next to her, the woman asks her
mother what I should do. I recognize her mother from my first day
volunteering in the cellar at the pagoda: she is Tín's wife, Hằng (Chapter 2). She remembers that I interviewed her husband the previous
summer and asks whether I plan to speak with more people.

When I confirm that I'm still looking for respondents, Hằng suggests that I go to the pagodas in the eastern part of the city where I
will find "different people" to interview. Nodding her head to the table
behind us, she advises me to ask the "northern brothers and sisters"
over there, who live in the east, and can show me the way. How disciples self-segregated in the pagoda thus reflects the boundedness of
the two migration streams before the fall of the Berlin Wall.[29] Even
as they attend pagoda together and move about in a shared physical
space, northerners and southerners remain apart in separate rooms or
at separate tables.

As is true of the travails of Anh and Hạnh in Chapter 5, people
who are neither refugees nor contract workers still find the coethnic
tension at the pagoda palpable. These include disciples born long after
the war ended. This was clear from my first day at Linh Thứu in 2014
as I met and spent time with the two teenaged volunteers. As soon
as we use up all of the ingredients to make dessert dough balls, we
begin to clean up. I carry trays to the sink, where one of the teenagers
washes them. Tall and gangly with long, straight hair, Anja introduces
herself to me in German. She is the daughter of southern refugees.
A minute later, Hanna, a shorter, heavier-set girl sporting a ponytail,
timidly joins. She is the daughter of a northern contract worker. Both
seventeen, they were born and raised in Berlin. As Anja takes some of
the clean trays to another room to store, I ask Hanna for suggestions
of places to go to meet Vietnamese people (người Việt).

Perhaps because of my accent, Hanna had assumed I wanted to
speak only to southerners. She recommends I ask around the pagoda because "the people here are mostly from the south, as are all
of the nuns." I clarify that I also want to speak with northerners. My
response seems to take some of the edge off, and the three of us, Anja

included, spend the rest of the afternoon together running errands for the nuns. We later retire in one of the guest rooms, stacked with bunk beds to host visitors from out of town. There, we rest and chat.

We weave through different topics before touching on relationships among Vietnamese border crossers in Germany, at which point Hanna notes in a low voice, "I think it's better if you don't ask about *chống cộng sản* [anticommunism]." I had been deliberately avoiding the phrase. Anja, who does not speak Vietnamese as well as Hanna, does not understand. Hanna translates what she said into German for Anja, explaining that she has heard it from time to time in the pagoda and finds that it really upsets people. "What about for you and your family?" I ask Hanna, because they come from the north. She answers that it is not really important for them but, directing her gaze at the floor, whispers, "For the [southern] boat people, it is." She continues,

There was a reporter, and she wanted to write about the disputes between north and south Vietnamese, but people did not want to speak with her, because they didn't want to be named.

(*Es gab eine Reporterin, und sie möchte über das Streiten zwischen Nord- und Süd-Vietnamesen schreiben, aber die Leute wollten nicht mit ihr sprechen, weil sie nicht genannt sein möchten.*)

Anja knows far less about these circumstances than Hanna does but nevertheless grasps the regional divide. When the three of us meet again two days later, Anja confesses that her mother does not socialize with northerners at the pagoda: "No, to be honest, she's quite prejudiced against them." She uses a Vietnamese word I am not sure about, so I offer a synonym: *tham lam*? Yes, she nods that she meant greedy. I ask where she thought that idea came from. "I'm not really sure," she replies. "It's like something really bad happened in the past or something and [my mom] just really doesn't like [northerners]." "Something like . . . a civil war?" I offer, tongue-in-cheek. "Yes!" she agrees, wagging her finger as if to signal, "Aha!"

As is true of their parents, second-generation northern Vietnamese Germans who talked about the war seemed reticent, at times even embarrassed. Hanna and I returned privately to the subject the next day as we finished our volunteer duties and headed out from the pagoda together. I asked, "When you told me not to ask people about anticommunism, how did you hear about all of that?" (*Khi em nói chị đừng nên hỏi người ta về chuyện chống cộng sản, làm sao em đã nghe qua về chuyện đó?*) Her gaze averted, she murmured in response, "I don't mean to speak badly about anyone. But it just makes me sad that there aren't very many northerners at pagoda." (*Em không thích nói xấu ai, nhưng em chỉ thấy hơi buồn là không có nhiều người bắc ở chùa thôi.*) Hanna's reluctant admission makes clear that southerners' anticommunism makes at least some northerners uncomfortable in the shared space.

Cold War Coreligionists

When scholars note tension among religious coethnics, they focus on competing belief systems;[30] this chapter instead shows how historical developments have politicized group boundaries among coethnics who share a religion. In the space of Linh Thứu Pagoda, attendees must reconcile their sense of shared identity around "race, ethnicity, religion, and nationality [all of which] are social constructions which typically have roots in long-standing self-conceptions of community."[31] The disciples at Linh Thứu spoke of and saw themselves as one people with coethnics from different migration streams and regions of origin. They acted on this sense of shared nationhood, such as when refugees reached out to contract workers after the fall of the Berlin Wall even while some refugees resented contract workers. As conflict over competing flags intensified, the nuns pushed for a reconciliation among the disciples who remained at the pagoda. The end result was that those who wanted to stay ceased bringing nationalist symbols into the religious space.

Others retained strong political beliefs in their everyday lives but put them aside at their pagodas for different reasons. For Lan, who used to cross over into East Germany to visit Viên Giác Pagoda, Buddhism helped her stop resenting individual communists, northerners, and former contract workers. After all, as she confided one night as we stayed up late talking, "good communists" need a chance to oppose Vietnam as well. Lan was one of the rare individuals I spent time with who attended protests and has refused to set foot back in Vietnam since her departure more than thirty years ago.

By contrast, former contract workers Huệ and Sơn had no need to reconcile their northern nationalisms with Buddhism at the eastern pagodas, which de facto supported their stances. Their national allegiances and religion did not conflict because the eastern pagodas were neither founded nor populated by southerners. In the absence of competing nationalist claims at the eastern pagodas, Huệ and Sơn emphasized shared religion. They denigrated the southerners for creating problems. Yet Huệ would not have taken offense at her pagoda flying the red flag; she only reacted when pagodas displayed the *wrong* flag.

The national allegiances of Lan, on one hand, and Huệ and Sơn, on the other, are not only competing but also incongruent. Lan rejects the Vietnamese state but still advocates a politics of ethnic nationalism. Among my interviewees, she alone clung vehemently to the hope that the communist regime could be toppled and the entire country converted to some version of the former South. She still subscribed to ethnic nationalism, albeit under a different flag. Most people I spoke with, however, had accepted that reunification under communism was a forgone conclusion. They did not hold out hope for an alternative anticommunist Vietnamese nation-state. Instead, they had forsaken the political project of ethnic nationalism.

Unlike Lan, Huệ and Sơn perceive ruptures in ethnic nationalism even though both accept the outcome of reunification, and even as one of them is ideologically committed to communism. Huệ and Sơn viewed southerners who dredged up the past as unnecessarily creating friction among a nation otherwise reunified. Both emphasized that "south and north are one house [family]" (*nam bắc [là] một nhà*) and should not differentiate among themselves. They insisted that southerners should accept that reunification already happened, and by accession of the South; this mirrors the relationship of West Germans to East Germans.[32] The former North's image of Vietnam came to encompass the entire territory and therefore to represent the reunified nation. To Huệ and Sơn, Southern nationalism should not intrude on the pagoda because it represents a vision of Vietnam that is already lost. Yet northerners like Huệ and Sơn also recognized that the expression of Southern nationalism discounts ethnic nationalism. They see southerners as fundamentally rejecting reunification rather than just reunification under a particular political direction. They thus interpreted demands for Southern nationalist spaces as a rejection of the political project of one nation, one state.

As Huệ's and Sơn's defections from the western pagoda suggest, religion does not successfully compete with or replace nationalism. Instead, the factionalisms grow to involve "religion" and the "religious"—already "essentially contested categories of practice."[33] This suggests an underpinning political, rather than strictly religious, source of conflict.

Political divisions therefore mapped onto religious life, but the latter also produced its own dynamics that challenge and reshape the political. On the one hand, disciples drew on the teachings of their faith to transcend the divisions they inherited from the multiple Cold War border crossings through which they had lived. On the other hand, they also used religion and religious difference as fodder to affirm in-group and out-group membership. These coethnic coreligionists pulled secular hostilities into a sacred space that they see as prizing unity. Vietnamese lay worshippers thereby demonstrate how different arenas of social life become absorbed into political divisions after border crossings. In the conclusion that follows, we return to the broader question of how these border crossings transform ethnic nationalism in quotidian, enduring ways.

7

After Border Crossings

DECADES AFTER THE COLD WAR, the identity labels of northerner and southerner, contract worker and refugee, communist and anticommunist all continue to inform how Vietnamese border crossers in Berlin interact with one another. This was evident on my last day at Linh Thứu Buddhist Pagoda in August 2016, when the entire ensemble of nuns in residence were joined by hundreds of lay worshippers and monks from Viên Giác Pagoda in Hanover. They gathered to celebrate Vu Lan, a Buddhist holiday that honors parents. Both the yellow-striped flag of South Vietnam and the red flag of the reunified Vietnam were absent. Only one flag waved above our heads that sunny day: the vertical striped international Buddhist flag. Kim, the international student from central Vietnam who shares an apartment with Hồng, performed with other young women as dragon dancers rested nearby. (See Figure 7.1.)

The setting was familiar enough: crowds of lay worshippers greeted their spiritual leaders and one another in northern and southern accents, a vegetarian feast awaiting all. Like other major holidays, this event seemed to promise coethnic unity. Beneath the veneer, however, the presence of monks from Viên Giác Pagoda evoked the Cold War era when followers of the fledgling Linh Thứu Pagoda had

Figure 7.1 Vu Lan musical performance at Linh Thứu Pagoda, August 2016. Source: Author.

to make intimidating trips through the East to reach the rest of West Germany for holiday celebrations. Despite the collapse of the Berlin Wall, current visitors to the pagoda still largely self-segregated by region of origin and migration stream. Converging in the shared religious space, Vietnamese migrants in Berlin have achieved the division of the homeland.

The Border Within took as its starting point the conviction of everyday Vietnamese people in Berlin that their ethnic nation has been irreparably splintered. These protagonists and their stories have not only provided the foundation for this book; they have propelled the mode of knowledge it seeks to produce. During my first foray into ethnographic research over a decade ago, I voiced to a trusted adviser, Nguyễn-võ Thu-hương, my concern that were I not careful enough, my interlocutors would find their narratives distorted in my writing.

I wanted to faithfully represent the memories with which I was en-
trusted, I told her. She wisely observed that there is a degree of inevitable alienation between the stories we collect and how our profession
demands that we present those findings, which often render them
indecipherable to the very people they claim to portray. One of my
central ambitions for this book has been to interpret the conversations
I shared with individuals, families, and groups in ways that faithfully
resonate with the ethos in which we passed much time together.

This study of everyday life returned again and again to how,
through their routine words and actions, people keep political boundaries alive. This, despite the fact that the geopolitical developments
associated with these boundaries have long since changed. For many
former refugees, their family members, and later arrivals who identify
with Southern nationalism, their rousing rhetoric bares the depth of
loss of a homeland to which they will never return. Indeed, it is one to
which they cannot return even when they set foot in the territory of
Vietnam, because South Vietnam is gone. This impossibility of return
is precisely what "instill[s] a need to stage a return to the war's history
again and again."[1] Former contract workers, their family members,
and latter arrivals recognize this as well. They note the impasse between their desire for unity within the ethnic nation and their percep-
tion that border crossings had permanently extracted some from the
bounds of the ethnic nation-state.

A sense of nationhood based on ethnicity may not matter to
everyone all the time, but it certainly did much of the time to the
Vietnamese subjects of this book. My focus on issues of local significance to ordinary people reminds us that although "an ethnicity bias
has skewed our interpretation of diverse social phenomena in the
world . . . the world which we study very often also *has* an ethnicity
bias."[2] From this basis, it has been challenging to balance my desire
to not assume "groupness" with my emphasis on what is meaningful
to people on the ground.[3] Methodologically, I sought to address this
by speaking to people "lost to the group,"[4] such as those who do not
participate in ethnic associations. (I had limited success in this regard
aside from Liên and Hải.) Analytically, I interrogated the categories of

northerner and southerner, refugee and contract worker, to show the slippage between these seemingly straightforward regional and migration labels. Even as this book examines the reproduction of ethnic nationhood and nationalism, then, it seeks to denaturalize ethnicity by charting the creation of ethnonational categories and highlighting when people think, identify, and act outside the bounds of the ethnic nation-state. I treat ethnicity as "the phenomenon to be explained, not to do the explaining with."[5] Here, I have presented a fractured Vietnamese ethnicity, where the fissures are exposed by the labels of north/south, contract worker/refugee, labels created by the twin border crossings people have experienced.

More broadly, I have asserted that by looking at people crossing borders and borders crossing people in tandem, we glean insights otherwise missed when we examine state formation and international migration separately. By looking at Vietnamese who border-cross to Western liberal democracies, we might see "long-distance" nationalists inciting operations in the homeland from afar.[6] By looking at Vietnamese who cross borders into countries of the former Eastern Bloc, we might see diasporans engaged in state-linked activities, including of those loyal to the Vietnamese homeland and state.[7] This book looks instead at the one location where border-crossed and border-crossing Vietnamese individuals relate above all else to one another. And how they do so reveals that they continue to believe in and act on a subjective sense of ethnic nationhood but have cast off the politics of ethnic nationalism.

Resoundingly, the Vietnamese subjects of this book have come to reject the political principle of one nation, one state. By aligning their Southern nationalism with the German nation-state, refugees have expanded their notions of belonging beyond the ethnic nation. Contract workers and later border crossers similarly see their refugee coethnics as part of the cultural, ethnic nation, but outside the nation-state. These coethnics have fulfilled the division of the homeland, ironically, decades after its reunification and outside its territory.

This book has been consumed with what we learn from encounters between people and borders, encounters among coethnics, and the divisions that such encounters reveal. This exercise in analytically informed storytelling reveals how encounters radically transform identities and practices on the ground. For Black schoolchildren in Kentucky, interracial encounters in desegregating US schools challenged the Jim Crow racial logics that claimed they were inferior to White children.[8] People moving within the realm of the Japanese Empire encountered legal and bureaucratic structures that revealed their difference as "Koreans" rather than just Japanese nationals.[9] It is precisely these encounters that reveal division.

Yet it is also division that keeps coethnics connected.[10] Encounters between officers in the Berlin police force after 1990, for example, exposed how political reunification did not lead to social reunification. At the point of reunification, they become "divided in unity."[11] Examining Vietnamese people's everyday understandings and practices of the nation, we see how a commitment to ethnic nationhood can persist even as people desert the political project of making the ethnic nation and state congruent.

Border crossings have long afterlives, and this book has invited readers to peer into such afterlives through the lens of Vietnamese people's day-to-day routines and interactions in Berlin. We can also draw from contemporary instances that similarly affirm the long-term impact of border crossings. As of my initial drafting in summer 2020, protests rage across the United States over the Confederate flag and statues. Perhaps less well known is that nationalist symbols of the Confederate States of America also find expression in Brazil, where thousands of defeated Southerners flocked when the Confederacy fell.[12] The descendants of these border crossers, known as *confederados*, decorate the cemetery that holds the remains of veterans, wear Confederate gray uniforms at commemorations, and name their children after General Robert E. Lee. The Confederacy existed for four years, but its symbols have lived on for more than 150 abroad.

Like South Vietnamese nationalists, confederados highlight how migrants carry political ideas and practices with them across borders. To be sure, the Confederacy differed from South Vietnam in significant ways. The Confederacy was not internationally recognized as a sovereign state, for one, whereas South Vietnam was. There are nevertheless uncanny echoes in the ways that defeated Southerners, both American and Vietnamese, transplanted their nationalist symbols and practices onto new soil. This echo between South Vietnam and the Confederacy has manifested in more volatile ways since I first wrote this conclusion, with Vietnamese American protesters waving the flag of South Vietnam during the US Capitol insurrection in January 2021. Looking at Vietnamese coethnics abroad exposes us to fault lines that might still endure in Vietnam but that have far fewer opportunities for expression there because northerners and southerners have not converged in one city as they have in Berlin.

The Border Within has thus traced how international migration weaves societies together, even as these interwoven societies have already been internally fractured by state formation. Wedged between decades of war, state formation in the homeland created internal enemies and heroes, producing nationals of unequal belonging. Border crossers then transplanted their stratified national memberships and attitudes about the home state across international borders. State formation in the host country bought these two border-crossing groups together in Berlin, allowing us to see how the idea of the ethnic nation informs everyday boundary-making processes even as people forsake an ethnonationalist project.

By looking at people caught in processes of state formation and international migration, this book affirms the importance of the nation-state in the lives of people who cross, and are crossed by, borders. Yet it also reveals something more surprising: even when we are repeatedly confronted with a profoundly felt sense of ethnic nationhood, we may nevertheless find that people have left the politics of ethnic nationalism behind.

Acknowledgments

This book is dedicated to my parents, Phan Thị Sen and Sử Khác Lợi, whose arduous border crossings smoothed the way for my own. It's fitting that they named me "to fly": it was their sacrifices, after all, that gave me wings.

For years, Phung N. Su has shouldered the often invisible labor that has allowed me to uproot time and again, knowing that our parents were cared for. I intend to repay this in kind as she writes her own book.

I have valued every part of this book writing process, above all, for the chance it gave me to forge human connections. I'm indebted foremost to the Vietnamese border crossers whose stories fill these pages. Walking archives of uncertainty, despair, joy, and everything in between, they offer powerful reminders of the resilience of the human spirit. *Phi xin cám ơn các bác cô chú anh chị em đã sắp xếp thời gian để chia sẻ câu chuyện của họ. Mặc dù tên thật của họ không xuất hiện ở đây, Phi sẽ luôn luôn nhớ ơn này.*

Đặc biệt, con muốn cám ơn Cô "Anh" cho sự nhiệt tình của cô.

In Berlin, Will and I were overwhelmed by the generosity of so many who helped us plant roots, later visited us in Los Angeles and the Gulf, showed us around their hometowns in Vietnam, and allowed us the honor of bearing witness to some of the biggest milestones of their lives. Bodo Bookhagen and Linda Juang, and Anja

Küppers-McKinnon and Kyle McKinnon opened up their homes to
us, offering a launching pad from which we could resume our Berlin adventures. Ha Phuong Le-Fitzek and Paulus Fitzek reliably asked
about the book over the years and made sure there was time to share
hot meals. Anh Thu Anne Lam took her charge as older sister in our
imagined family earnestly. I thank her for our conversations in mean-
dering tongues.

These and many more good folks made our return to Berlin in
2019 a homecoming. To ensure their confidentiality, I have omitted
the names of individuals and families whose stories appear in the
book. But I hope to have adequately conveyed how deeply I value
them in my life.

The data collection for this book was made possible by a fellowship
through the Berlin Program for Advanced German and European
Studies. As coordinator, Karin Goihl fiercely championed this project
and its architect.

In its earliest stages, this research benefited from feedback by Berlin Program colleagues and friends: Sultan Doughan, Claire Greenstein, and Brian Van Wyck. While juggling second and third shifts,
Sultan enthusiastically made time for conversations about our sib-
ling disciplines of anthropology and sociology. Claire inspired me to
write for public audiences and has brought her comparative politics
lens to this work. More important, I continue to learn so much from
her about kindness as an intentional practice. A committed educator,
Brian is one of the gentlest souls I have the pleasure to call my friend.
I thank him for lending me his historian's eye on several occasions.

Feng-Mei Heberer, I'm so glad we found each other at that Berlin
workshop years ago; our conversations have nourished my spirits in
much-needed times.

I previously published parts of this book in different forms.
Chapters 1, 2, and 3 include material from "Competing Contexts of
Reception in Refugee and Immigrant Incorporation: Vietnamese in
West and East Germany" (with Frank Bösch), *Journal of Ethnic and*

Migration Studies, available online first, and from "Vietnamesische Migration nach Westdeutschland: Ein Historischer Zugang" (with Christina Sanko), in *Unsichtbar: Vietnamesisch-Deutsche Wirklichkeiten* (Köln und Bonn: DoMiD and Friedrich-Ebert-Stiftung, 2017). My dependable coollaborators, Frank and Tina expanded this project's interdisciplinary horizons. I thank Rachel Gisselquist and Sascha Wölck for providing me the impetus to undertake these efforts. Chapter 4 includes vignettes that appear in "'There's No Solidarity': Nationalism and Belonging among Vietnamese Refugees and Immigrants in Berlin," *Journal of Vietnamese Studies* 12, no. 1: 73–100. I thank Christina Schwenkel for the invitation to pursue this piece.

During graduate studies, I refined my language abilities through funding from the German Academic Exchange Program and US Department of Education's Foreign Language and Area Studies Fellowships for German and Vietnamese.

Fifteen years ago, this project was but a hodgepodge of my wanderlust and interests in Germany, until Mary Kunmi Yu Danico gave it a push. When *Kyosunnim* first suggested I apply to graduate school, I laughed incredulously. I was the daughter of working-poor refugees, and no one in my family had yet graduated from college. *Kyosunnim*'s confidence that I could pursue an academic career and the resources she marshaled toward this end changed my life. Everything I know about social justice—about community-building, professionalism, the life-changing possibilities of mentorship, and a radical politics of love—I first learned from you. What an inheritance you've given me. Because of you, I will always be a proud product of a California public education that labors to transform the lives of underrepresented students.

At Cal Poly Pomona, I developed a love of sociology alongside Jessica M. Kizer and Jessica C. Moronez, fellow McNair Scholars who have embarked on their own academic careers. My oldest friends, if I ever start to take myself too seriously, your embarrassing memories of our teenage years should help me cut that shit out.

No word in the English language seems to do justice to what Rubén Hernández-León has been as a *Doktorvater*. It is to you I owe my greatest intellectual debt. Thank you for reminding me to match rigor with accessibility, and a commitment to teaching with an equal one to research in the conviction that they mutually strengthen each other. "Thank you" does not sufficiently express the role you played as my first and most committed advocate at UCLA, and that you still continue to play as the Rubenitos' namesake. Above all, you model for me that intellectual heroes can and should also be exemplary human beings.

As the third installment of the Rubenitos book empire, this book gained immensely from the two that preceded. While completing their own books, Tahseen Shams and Eli Revelle Yano Wilson joined me on this book's journey as accountability buddies. Tahseen freely shared every tip she painstakingly collected, and her feedback has reshaped my outlook toward writing. My fiercely loyal friend, how I've cherished our bond. Eli and I have long shared a love of food and unpretentious prose. I hope you see some of those shared commitments, strengthened with your feedback, reflected in these pages.

My appreciation for my sociology mentors as UCLA has only deepened in the years since I graduated. I'm overcome with how invested they've been in my well-being and successes, as a human being before all else. I can always count on Gail Kligman's detailed commentary on my work as well as on the state of the world, an important reminder that we do not write in a vacuum. I continue to be in awe of Roger Waldinger's untiring curiosity and commitment to mentoring, which has only ramped up as the pandemic has raged. I look to Min Zhou as an exemplar of a healthy work-life balance who has also seamlessly threaded home across multiple locations.

For their intellectual and affective support as I developed the dissertation on which this book is based, I am particularly grateful to Deisy Del Real, Lauren Duquette-Rury, Andrew Le, Saskia Nauenberg Dunkell, Vilma Ortiz, Christopher M. Rea, Casandra Salgado, Whitney Richards-Calathes, and Amy Zhou.

As a dissertation accountability buddy, Calvin Ho would not tolerate bad writing. I know he adores me enough to overlook whatever jargon remains, and I thank him for traipsing three continents to be with me and Will.

When we last returned to LA as visitors, Juan Delgado and Leydy Diossa-Jimenez gave us a home. Two of the most pleasant people I know, I look forward to celebrating all of their milestones, as they have mine.

Outside of the Department of Sociology, Nguyễn-võ Thu-hương and David K. Yoo provided me an intellectual home in Asian and Asian American Studies. As the resident expert on Vietnam, memory, and violence, Thu-hương could so easily have intimidated me. She never did, though, because she works to build up junior scholars and help them advance on their own terms. David knows full well the labor it takes to forge and sustain connections, yet he never shies from pouring his energies toward these admirable goals. I'm fortunate to have had such wonderful Asian American role models, so much so that I at times take for granted that not all are so lucky.

As a family of young academics, Will and I made the best decision of our lives to come to New York University Abu Dhabi (NYUAD). This book would not have been possible without the time, resources, and interdisciplinary community that the university offered.

David Cook-Martín was my first point of contact with the institution, and I'm so glad he recruited me. Thank you for helping me demystify this trade.

When David moved back to the United States, I looked to Rebecca Morton to supervise me. Although we had no research overlaps, I trusted Becky to have my best interests in mind and to muster the strength needed to overcome the bureaucracies that confront newcomers everywhere. With her sudden passing, countless junior scholars have lost an incredible ally. I only hope to pay forward some of the advocacy she modeled.

Etienne Wasmer stepped into the gaping hole left by Becky's absence and has steadfastly worked toward the well-being of the postdoctoral community. I thank him for conversations about interdisciplinarity and navigating this great and peculiar profession.

And despite her taxing load as Interim Dean, Hannah Brückner gave generously of her time to strategize about my future as an individual and as part of a family. We thank her for providing Will the chance to design his dream course, and for entrusting me with Senior Capstone.

John O'Brien was one of the first smiling faces to welcome me to Abu Dhabi. While balancing his newfound duties as Program Head, he also made time to help me navigate the final stretch of this book process.

I have learned much from being part of the Capstone team with John, Eric Hamilton, Saba Karim Khan, and Marouane Laouina. In particular, I have valued the opportunity to co-teach with Saba, visual anthropologist, public writer extraordinaire, ally, and kindred spirit. I welcome many more opportunities to co-create together.

I'm convinced I had some of the best students in the world. As I completed revisions to this book, Saba's and my capstone section was knee-deep in carrying out impressively multimethodological, multisited research on pressing social issues. Amna AlShamsi, Amina Bašić, Lucas Davidenco, Mariam El Sheikh, Misa Morikawa, Nejat Mussa, Lulu Zakia Qonita, Maira Sheikh, Yao Xu, and Haewon Yoon: you have each inspired me with your resilience and good nature in the face of uncertainty. It has been my privilege to be your teacher. I'm hopeful for all of the ways you will go on to spread good in the world.

In particular, I'm grateful that Mariam asked me to advise her capstone project, and I'm moved by her commitment to amplify voices of Nubian displacement. Yao, fellow cat lover, R whiz, and delightful coauthor: I welcome the opportunity to call you a sociology colleague and dear friend one day soon.

Frieda Luna Schlör lent her impressive skill set to this book; I thank her for the maps she carefully furnished.

At the Hilary Ballon Center for Teaching and Learning, Nancy W. Gleason has been a treasure trove of pedagogical insight. She moved me to think more deeply about the craft of teaching and to reflect those commitments in my research.

I have loved being part of a small campus community, where the same SERCO colleagues who greeted me when I walked into A5 each morning (in the Before Times) also schooled me on the badminton courts later that evening. I have an incurable need to plant roots, and have so appreciated the social science admin team for being some of the finest tenders of this transplanted garden. I thank Flora Alipio, Sima Basel, Alizeh Batra, Caroline Kassab, Janet Kelly, Marta Martinez Collada, Julie McGuire, and Diana Pangan for indulging my Broadway serenades (however off-key) and for the warmth you all brought to A5. The only way to have a Yemeni feast is with kind souls such as yourselves. *Ate* Flora and Alizeh, how I'll miss our hallway chatter and giggles.

Colleagues and friends in the Division of Social Science have filled the last few years with insight, humor, and good food. I thank Elisabeth Anderson, Swethaa Ballakrishnen, Rosemary Byrne, Georgi Derluguian, Romain Ferrali, Sabino Kornrich, Kangsan Lee, Rabia Malik, Rana Tomaira, and Didem Türkoğlu for their engagement with my work.

When strict lockdown came to Abu Dhabi, Romain Germain Hugues Gauriot lent us his apartment so that we could have an occasional change of scenery. I look forward to when we can go fruit picking together with him and Claire-Louise Salles again.

Yaoyao Dai, my wonderfully quirky twin: you spark so much joy. I will miss our in-person shenanigans with Alexandra Blackman and Giuliana Pardelli. Giuli generously opened up her home to us in the last stretch of our time in Abu Dhabi. Until we can safely gather again, I look forward to every Zoom chat and ACNH island visit.

I may well have been more productive in this postdoc position were it not for the Romains, Yaoyao, Alex, Giuli, Sergio Ascencio, Renae Hesse, Javier Mejía, Georgia Michailidou, and Marc Witte, as well as my food group buddies, Aaron Chow, Jixing Li, Michael Mehari, Jiranuwat (Bas) Sapudom, and Kendra Strouf. But I would undoubtedly have enjoyed myself far less.

Manu Muñoz-Herrera and Sharlane Muñoz Scheepers, your appreciation for life and your openness to new experiences will buoy us as we undertake our next border crossing and work to rebuild home once more.

Tuomo Tiisala, Will and I have so valued the care with which you've approached this friendship. We know time will only strengthen this connection.

For years, Elena Korchmina was my confidante and cheerleader. I treasure the many hours we stole away in 1101 and on the highline, chatting away about everything under the sun.

Since we've moved to Zoom, I know whenever I see May Al-Dabbagh's name pop up that I will have a co-conspirator there who is committed to elevating voices that are often discounted and to interrogating whose worldviews we take as rigorous. I treasure you.

To paraphrase the wise Eman Abdelhadi, when we leave a place, we leave behind not only people and institutions but versions of ourselves. All of our dear ones in Abu Dhabi have shaped this version of our family—a more open, adventurous, and joyful version that we hope will carry us to our next home.

In the process of transforming this manuscript from its earlier incarnation as a dissertation, I am thrilled to have had Marcela Maxfield at Stanford University Press steer me through to the finish line. She gave vital feedback on the book's narrative flow early on and has curated a far more positive experience of first-time book publishing than I could have asked for. Sunna Juhn expertly moved this book through to production. I thank Stephanie Adams, Emily Smith, Beverly Miller, and the many more folks at SUP who will sculpt this book into its physical form over the coming months.

Two anonymous reviewers offered generative and careful feedback. Their comments pushed me to elevate the stakes of this book, all the while centering on what I wanted to achieve.

This publication is made possible by the generous support of the NYU Abu Dhabi Grants for Publication Program. As I prepared this book for initial submission, a first grant allowed me to work with Helen Glenn Court. I thank Glenn for tightening up the prose on my initial submission and for teaching me some good writing tips in the process. A second grant offset further costs for the final manuscript, including photo permissions and indexing.

The final drafts of this book benefited from incisive feedback by Zeynep Ozgen, Christopher Paik, Leonid Peisakhin, and Mustafa Yavas. Years ago in front of Luvalle Commons at UCLA, Zeynep urged me to think about my work not just as a case of international migration but of nationalism. There's a satisfying parallel to having her sharp mind on this book's framework of dual border crossings a decade later. My cycling and badminton buddy, fellow food fanatic, and *ahjusshi*, Chris: it's been a hoot. We'll find other places to resume sports, food, laughter, and solidarity. I am inspired by Leo's penetrating insights: he's a thinker who processes your jumbled thoughts and bounces back a summary or phrase that perfectly captures what you've struggled to explain. Mustafa is as gracious and deliberate when giving feedback as when he receives it. I'm eager to return the favor and support him on his book. These folks make the NYUAD Division of Social Science intellectual gold.

One of the biggest perks of this profession for me has been the chance to connect with folks whose intellectual projects I've found deeply inspiring. It is in this spirit that I extend my appreciation to Olga Dror and Jaeeun Kim, who trained their expertise on this book's historical and analytical claims. I hope they find their time and efforts rewarded. Any remaining errors of fact or analysis remain stubbornly my own.

At the NYUAD Scientific Writing Program, Philip Rodenbough read every chapter of this final submission. I thank him for his reminders about meta-discourse and elegant writing as well as for the positivity with which has always responded to my work.

With just days to go before our departure from Abu Dhabi, Hannah Brückner has come through for this book and its author yet again, making the book trailer possible. I'm grateful to Aleksandar Sandarov, Joseph Pritchard, and their team at We Are Alive Animation Studio for taking on this project, and to Rebecca Pittam for sneaking me into the NYUAD recording studio just in the nick of time.

As Count Rugen deadpanned to Prince Humperdink: "If you haven't got your health, you haven't got anything." It in this spirit that I extend my gratitude to my medical support unit. While I plugged away at this book. Dr. Rashid Hassen at the International Chiropractic Specialty Center worked to undo years of bad academic posture and work habits. I thank him for our conversations about spinal health, politics, and, most of all, the lives of people on the move. I will continue to badger everyone I know to stand up every thirty minutes. In the midst of a global pandemic, Dr. Monica Singh Chauhan and Nurse Alexandria Cortez at Burjeel Hospital remained committed to excellent gynecological care. At the Cleveland Clinic Abu Dhabi, Dr. Mohsen Nasir kept watch on my respiratory health, always with a sense of humor and a dash of sarcasm. Finally, Dr. Ivana Romac Coc and her team expertly remade my vision. More than ever, I'm convinced that health and self-care are necessary, revolutionary acts.

As I wrapped up graduate studies, Williams College provided my first venue for presenting a near-completed dissertation. I walked into Sawyer Library a ball of nerves, but relaxed once I saw Joel Lee's beaming face in the audience. I remain inspired by you as a colleague, educator, and good soul and thank you for the fire you lit for me to return to book writing.

No better colleague have I ever known than Christina Simko. I have so treasured having you on this journey with me. You understood so deeply and advocated for exactly the vision I had for the book. And you held space when the social problems we as sociologists often write about hit too close to home. My heart is full with how much I have received from you.

I can't think of a more rewarding way to see this book come into the world than in Williamstown with both of you and other colleagues I'm sure Will and I will come to know and cherish. We are delighted to be joining you very soon.

Finally, my chosen family has kept my spirits high throughout the past few years and even more so as the pandemic took hold.

Maria Grigoryeva and Michelle O'Brien, this sisterhood kept me afloat in the dark days of 2020. I'm grateful for the physically distanced pod we built. And it's amazing to me that even the most recently invented traditions can carry so much gravity: we will sorely miss holiday dinners with the little Grigoryevas and Blaine Robbins (aka "TUV").

Rahim Kurwa and I have talked just about every week for years and have grown (wiser, I hope) together even as we no longer occupy a shared space. I value the constant role you've played in my life.

Malte Reichelt, badminton archnemesis, fellow cat and food obsessive, and beloved *Kumpel*: the world truly needs more Maltes. Your friendship makes my heart soar.

Chris Walker, only you would let us navigate you into a Moroccan souk and make the fifty-point turn needed to escape without skipping a beat. Whatever fiascos we get into next, we'll overcome them together with patience and a lot of love. We always build home with you in mind.

Finally, the heartbeat of our mobile family unit is Will Stahl, with whom I've stitched home across three continents. This book is dedicated to my parents, this life to you. You still fill every moment with endless joy.

Abu Dhabi
June 2021

Appendix: Research Notes

To hone my central argument about how border crossings shape ethnic nationhood and nationalism, I sacrificed other threads that run through the ethnographic narratives of the book. The first example of this has to do with gender. Each empirical chapter of this book hinted at how "state power, citizenship, nationalism, militarism, revolution, political violence, dictatorship, and democracy—are all best understood as masculinity projects, involving masculine institutions, masculine processes and masculine activities."[1] For example, everyday people interpreted the division of Vietnam after the Battle of Dien Bien Phu through the lens of war and fallen soldiers, whom they, by default, imagined as men. Boat people refugees fleeing Vietnam in the late 1970s were also overwhelmingly boys and men, and we can think of their forced displacement as presenting a crisis of masculinity.[2] But women also left Vietnam to go abroad, including as contract workers and marriage migrants. Their gendered border-crossing pathways would influence their family dynamics. Furthermore, it was women who sought to insert themselves in both northern and southern cultural spaces and who were penalized for attempting to do so. It was women who performed the work of maintaining religious sites and who outwardly criticized the religious practices of others. But although I show how *men* or *women* perform certain functions and roles, I do not elaborate how *gender* shapes and is shaped by border crossings. Instead, I have looked to scholarship that has addressed the

nation as a profoundly gendered construct,[3] and international migration as inextricably informed by gender as well.[4]

Second, by centering the act of border crossing rather than specific types of border crossers, this book implicitly melds together the
insights of socialist mobilities and critical refugee studies. It does so
by shifting emphasis away from border crossings to Western capitalist contexts, where scholars and policymakers have focused much of
their attention,[5] and comparing such movements with flows among
socialist states. Before the fall of the Eastern Bloc, socialist countries
engaged in vibrant networks of exchange involving students, trainees,
experts, and workers. These networks reveal how "mobility was in fact
key to the realization of socialist international ideology,"[6] with people
on the move signaling the solidarity of global socialism. And just as
the figure of the socialist worker bolstered the image of socialist countries, the figure of the refugee also reinforced the legitimacy of capitalist countries. As critical refugee scholars keenly observe, refugees
played a crucial role in propping up the image of the United States as
a place that could provide refuge after its stunning defeat in Vietnam.[7]
Comparing different kinds of border crossers, then, reveals the power
of the state, more broadly, in deciding who is worthy of protection
and solidarity, whose presence threatens to sully the body politic,[8] and
how these labels of deservingness—however problematic—inform
people's social identities and relations.

Third, I concentrated on first-generation border crossers rather
than on their children. I did spend time with 1.5- and second-
generation Vietnamese Germans, as well as young, newly arriving
border crossers. But I did not focus, for example, on how their time
in school or other social spheres may have shaped their experiences
of citizenship and identity. Such a focus would also draw more attention to the German context and how schools, peers, or sporting events
transmit understandings of the nation. I'm heartened by the fact that
1.5- and second-generation Vietnamese Germans and their colleagues
are seizing this task, and take this opportunity to direct the curious
reader to projects such as *Ist Zuhause da, wo die Sternfrüchte süß sind?*

[*Is Home Where the Starfruit Is Sweet?*] and relatedly to the Free University of Berlin's Affective Societies project.

Finally, while I focus on international border crossings, the insights of this book might travel well to border crossings that happen within a nation-state.[9] We can think, for example, of people living in present-day Syria as border-crossed, when their homes and neighborhoods revert to one competing faction or another depending on the course of battle. The ongoing war has also driven people to cross borders into other cities and towns, where they are internally displaced. The lessons of this book would suggest that Syrian people who cross, and are crossed by, internal borders will grapple with questions of belonging and national allegiances for years to come.[10]

I hope that *The Border Within* will inspire further theorizing on how both types of border crossings jointly illuminate social processes. First, border crossings reflect and produce gendered social identities and behaviors. Second, border crossings further suggest that the central figure of the migrant—rather than the refugee or socialist worker as particular types of migrants—reveals broader transformative processes. Third, border crossings shape how the next generation(s) in turn negotiate the afterlives of state formation and international migration. Finally, border crossings and their insights may well travel beyond this book's focus on international borders.

Notes

Preface

1. In Vietnamese, pronouns such as *I* and *you* take on kinship terms that signal gender and relative age.

2. Malešević 2019, 39.

3. Pinkel 2010.

4. The "1.5ers" are those born abroad but raised in the United States from a young age.

5. Espiritu 2014.

6. Sebastian Schubert, "Berlin's Vietnamese Wall," *Deutsche Welle*, November 27, 2004, https://www.dw.com/en/berlins-vietnamese-wall/a-1408694.

7. Borneman 1992, 57.

8. Kate Connolly, "'Germany Looks Like It's Still Divided': Stark Gaps Persist 30 Years after Reunification," *The Guardian*, September 16, 2020, https://www.theguardian.com/world/2020/sep/16/germany-east-west-gaps-persist-30-years-reunification; Dalton and Weldon 2010; Glaeser 2000; Marcel Fürstenau, "Germany Faces Old Problems 30 Years after Reunification," *Deutsche Welle*, October 3, 2020, https://www.dw.com/en/germany-reunification-2020/a-55131890; Nathan Stoltzfus, "30 Years after the Berlin Wall Came Down, East and West Germany Are Still Divided," *The Conversation*, November 10, 2019, https://theconversation.com/30-years-after-the-berlin-wall-came-down-east-and-west-germany-are-still-divided-126589.

9. Hobsbawm and Ranger 1983.

Chapter 1

1. Hồ Chí Minh proclaimed an independent Democratic Republic of Vietnam in 1945, but France continued to exert power over greater Indochina until 1954. The State of Vietnam existed from 1949 until 1955, when Ngô Đình

Diệm led a referendum to oust the ceremonial state of head, Bảo Đại, and establish the Republic of Vietnam.

2. Geneva Agreements Article 14(d). https://peacemaker.un.org/sites/peacemaker.un.org/files/KH-LA-VN_540720_GenevaAgreements.pdf.

3. Graziano 2017, 3–4.

4. FitzGerald and Arar 2018.

5. Hamlin 2021.

6. Ibid., 159.

7. Brubaker 1996.

8. Cisneros 2013, 4

9. Shevchenko 2015, 65.

10. I am indebted here to Christina Simko for capturing exactly what I was trying to do.

11. Besbris and Khan 2017.

12. Calhoun 1993, 216. Rogers Brubaker's *Citizenship and Nationhood in France and Germany* is the classic reference for ethnic nationhood. However, his "point is a structural one, not a social-psychological one." He does not suggest "that the sense of membership or 'identity' was primarily ethnocultural," but, rather, that the logics underpinning citizenship were (1992, 4–5). However, my point is a social one.

13. On countries (and their nations) as a club, see Keating 2018.

14. Gellner 2006, 1.

15. Fox and Miller-Idriss 2008, 536.

16. Breuilly 1993.

17. Kim 2014 refers specifically to diasporic nationhood.

18. Sebastian Schubert, "Berlin's Vietnamese Wall," *Deutsche Welle*, November 27, 2004, https://www.dw.com/en/berlins-vietnamese-wall/a-1408694.

19. Brubaker 1996.

20. Choate 2008.

21. Viet Thanh Nguyen, "There's a Reason the South Vietnamese Flag Flew during the Capitol Riot," *Washington Post*, January 14, 2021, https://www.washingtonpost.com/outlook/2021/01/14/south-vietnam-flag-capitol-riot/.

22. Dror 2018, 6, 9.

23. P. Bui 2003.

24. Lipman 2020, 64.

25. Ibid., 136, 170, 195.

26. Fox and Miller-Idriss 2008, 537, 540.

27. Billig 1995.

28. Scholars differ on the pace with which ethnicity changes. See Chandra 2006, 2012 for a discussion of why this is, beginning with the need to define what we mean when we say *ethnicity*.

29. Schubert, "Berlin's Vietnamese Wall."
30. Laitin 1998, 346.
31. Gordon 1964.
32. Choate 2008; Coutin 2007; Fitzgerald 2008; Waldinger 2015.
33. Marrow 2013.
34. Glick Schiller, Basch, and Szanton Blanc 1995.
35. Shams 2020.
36. Dreby 2010; R. Smith 2006.
37. Hernández-León 2008.
38. Spener 2009.
39. Hagan 1994.
40. Zhou and Bankston 1998.
41. Del Real 2019.
42. Surak 2012 refers to this as "intranational differences."
43. Wimmer 2008, 971.
44. Wimmer 2013, 204.
45. Shams 2020.
46. Graziano 2017, 40.
47. FitzGerald 2019; Pedraza 2007.
48. Eckstein 2009, 36.
49. Le and Su 2018.
50. Bösch and Su forthcoming.
51. Following Gordon 1964, earlier migration scholarship paid central heed to the role of the host state.
52. Waldinger 2015.
53. Pfaff 2006.
54. Sammartino 2010, 13. Nazi Germany also sought eastward expansion, but their plans for "the Germanization of those deemed 'Germanizable' (*eindeutschungsfähig*)" (Brubaker and Kim 2011: 31) aimed at ethnoracial purification, rather than at ethnonational solidarity.
55. Waldinger 2015, 6.
56. Haddad 2008.
57. Arendt 1966.
58. Valverde 2003, 2012.
59. Hearn and Antonsich 2018, 595.
60. Only one person, a second-generation child of a Vietnamese mother and German father, expressly did not identify as such. She agreed to speak with me anyway but clarified that "[she is,] however, not Vietnamese" (Ich bin aber keine Vietnamesin).
61. Kwon 2010.
62. Seol and Skrentny 2009.

Chapter 2

1. Taylor 2013, 398, 622.
2. Fall 1967, 41.
3. Marr 2004.
4. E. Miller 2013, 90.
5. Ibid., 2
6. Ibid., 6.
7. The agreements also established time for opposing forces to withdraw troops from either side of Vietnam, as well as from Laos and Cambodia.
8. E. Miller 2013, chaps. 3, 4.
9. Dror 2018, 168.
10. Nguyễn T. D. 2019, 741.
11. After Diệm's assassination, however, Southern actors largely "did not claim as their goal, nor did they attempt, an invasion of the North" (Dror 2018, 9).
12. Ibid., 71.
13. Chapman 2013; E. Miller 2013.
14. Verdery 1993, 43.
15. Fox and Idriss-Miller 2008, 536.
16. Meyer 2021, 260.
17. Słowiak 2019, 627.
18. Taylor 2013, 563.
19. Boot 2018, 54.
20. Hansen 2009, 185–186.
21. Shacknove 1985, 280.
22. Young 1991, 2.
23. Słowiak 2019, 625–626.
24. Trân T. L. 2005, 432.
25. Słowiak 2019, 626.
26. Keith 2012, chap. 6.
27. Hansen 2009, 187.
28. P. V. Nguyen 2016.
29. Hansen 2009, 184.
30. Northern migrants went on to high positions in Diệm's administration (Young 1991, 56). This led to accusations that the president showed favoritism toward northern Catholics (Taylor 2013, 586). However, historian Phi-Vân Nguyen argues that "Diệm never fully trusted the refugees" and dispersed them out of suspicion (2016, 213).
31. Hansen 2009, 201.
32. Taylor 2013, 585.

33. Keating 2018, 39.

34. A. Smith 1986, although see Chandra 2006, 2012.

35. Gellner 2006, 1.

36. Keating 2018, introduction.

37. Calhoun 1993, 216.

38. Malešević 2019.

39. Hardy 2001, 189.

40. Ibid., 189–190.

41. Leshkowich 2014, 151.

42. Bélanger and Khuât 1996, 89–90.

43. Leshkowich 2014, 159.

44. Hardy 2001, 189.

45. Kligman and Verdery 2011, 106.

46. Schwenkel 2015, 4.

47. Hardy 2001, 190.

48. Woodside 1970, 706.

49. Moise 1976, 73–78.

50. Taylor 2013, 571.

51. Kim 2016, 15.

52. Young 1991, 56.

53. Ibid., 62.

54. Nguyễn T. D. 2019, 741

55. Ibid.

56. Chapman 2013, 129.

57. Nguyễn T. D. 2019, 743.

58. Historian Nguyễn Thị Điểu notes that the "Anti-Communist Denunciation Campaign . . . was never referred to by name in any official Vietnamese government documents that the author has found. It was alluded to publicly only in staged street demonstrations by police forces, civil servants, and so forth" (2019, 736).

59. Hunt 2007, 45; Young 1991, 56; Taylor 2013, 563.

60. Chapman 2013, 144.

61. E. Miller 2013, 196–197.

62. Chapman 2013, 76.

63. Taylor 2013, 601.

64. Young 1991, 104.

65. Dror 2018, 58, 244.

66. Ibid., 244, 61.

67. Zolberg 1983.

68. Similarly, following the Tiananmen Square protests of 1989, the United States passed the Chinese Student Protection Act of 1992, which protected

Western-educated students from being deported to China and provided a pathway to legalization (Gao 2006).

69. Taylor 2013, 614.

70. Leshkowich 2014, 143.

71. Shacknove 1985, 276.

72. History.com, "South Vietnam Surrenders," April 30, 2009, http://www.history.com/this-day-in-history/south-vietnam-surrenders.

73. Toai 1980.

74. Metzner et al. 2001.

75. Pike 1981.

76. F. Brown 1995, 78–79.

77. Song Jing, "Vietnamese Refugees Well Settled in China, Await Citizenship," United Nations High Commissioner for Refugees, May 10, 2007, http://www.unhcr.org/en-us/news/latest/2007/5/464302994/vietnamese-refugees-well-settled-china-await-citizenship.html.

78. Zolberg 1983, 26.

79. Hamlin and Wolgin 2012, 618.

80. FitzGerald 2019.

81. Hamlin 2012, 961.

82. Shacknove 1985, 276.

83. I thank Christopher Paik for this observation.

84. Dror 2018, 7.

Chapter 3

1. In 1981 alone, 349 of 452 boats arriving in Thailand had been attacked three times each (United Nations High Commissioner for Refugees 2000, 87). More than five hundred women had been raped and two hundred abducted.

2. Overwhelmed by the influx of people for whom they did not want responsibility, several Southeast Asian countries prevented boats from disembarking beginning in the mid-1979.

3. They did so at the urging of regional actors such as Hong Kong, which ultimately succeeded in reversing the previous treatment of arriving "boat people" as de facto refugees (Lipman 2020, chap. 4).

4. Portes and Böröcz 1989; Portes and Rumbaut 2014.

5. In very rare instances when speaking to second-generation Vietnamese Germans, I asked, "*Könnten Sie bitte mir erzählen, wie Sie oder Ihre Eltern in dieses Land gekommen sind?*"

6. Dennis 2007.

7. "Hong Kong officials believed that northern Vietnamese were coming for economic reasons, and they implied that only southern Vietnamese could

be 'real refugees.' The United States too came to this conclusion, and as a rule, it did not resettle northern Vietnamese" (Lipman 2020, 170).

8. These included "the provinces of Nghe An, Quang Binh, Ha Tinh, Hai Phong, and the city of Hanoi" (Beadle and Davison 2019, 34).

9. Hamlin 2021, 155.

10. Espiritu 2014, 13.

11. Loescher and Scanlan 1986.

12. FitzGerald 2019.

13. Triadafilopoulous and Schönwälder 2006.

14. Schönwälder 2004, 249.

15. Green 2001, 89.

16. Hailbronner 1994; Klusmeyer 1993.

17. Portes and Rumbaut 2014, 139.

18. Brubaker 1992.

19. Portes and Böröcz 1989.

20. *"Da die »Cap Anamur« unter bundesdeutscher Flagge fuhr, war die Bundesrepublik formal verpflichtet, die schiffbrüchigen Flüchtlinge aufzunehmen"* (Bösch 2017, 30).

21. Beuchling 2008.

22. Vermerk Innenministerium Niedersachsen, August 20, 1985, in ACDP 01-473-029/8, cited in Bösch and Su 2018.

23. Government 1975 notice, in Bundesarchiv B 136 16709, cited in Bösch and Su 2018.

24. Hillmann 2005, 86; Wolf 2007, 4.

25. Zhou and Bankston 1998.

26. Ogbu 1987.

27. Kolinsky 2004, 85.

28. Surak 2017.

29. Schwenkel 2014, 239.

30. Elsner and Elsner 1992; Weiss 2005.

31. Dennis 2005.

32. Surak 2013, 90.

33. Cook-Martín 2019.

34. Klessmann 2011, 192.

35. Nearly half of the Vietnamese contract workers in Halle reportedly engaged in side jobs (Dennis 2007, 347).

36. Marrow 2013.

37. For more on panethnicity, see Espiritu 1992; Okamoto and Mora 2014.

38. Hunt 2007, chap. 6.

39. "During the ten-year bilateral agreement, women constituted about 37 per cent . . . of Vietnamese employees" (Dennis 2007, 341).

40. Catholic refugees also reported going out to help their coethnics during this time, but Linh Thứu Buddhist Mindfulness Road members provided most firsthand reports of coordinated efforts.

41. Hamlin 2021, 4.

42. "Die deutsche Wiedervereinigung bedeutete für die vietnamesischen Vertragsarbeiten den außerdem vor allem Unsicherheit" (VLab Berlin 2020, 13).

43. P. Bui 2003.

44. Kolinsky 2004, 97.

45. Ha 2014.

46. Beuchling 2008.

47. Portes and Böröcz 1989.

48. Hillmann 2005.

49. Colloquially, she pronounced five as *lăm*, but it is written *năm*.

50. Hillmann 2005, 92.

51. Wolf 2007, 8.

52. Kolinsky 2004, 84.

53. FitzGerald 2019, 29.

54. Hillmann 2005, 92.

55. These estimates also assume that true refugees are rare. But as Rebecca Hamlin argues, "[T]here are very large numbers of people who deserve compassion and assistance, and . . . it can be confoundingly difficult to work out which ones should get priority" (2021, 155).

56. FitzGerald 2019, 3.

57. Menjívar 2006; Korntheuer, Pritchard, and Maehler 2017, 39.

58. Mehrländer, Ascheberg, and Ueltzhöffer 1996.

59. Wolf 2007, 9.

60. Stepick and Stepick 2009.

61. Itzigsohn and Saucedo 2002.

62. For a demographic overview, see Bösch and Su forthcoming.

63. Kocaturk-Schuster et al. 2017.

64. For more on war, debt, and refugeehood, see M. T. Nguyen 2012.

65. Fox 2003, 462.

Chapter 4

1. When quotations appear without the original Vietnamese or German, I had jotted down the phrase as quickly as possible after leaving the site.

2. Fox and Miller Idriss 2008, 540.

3. Brubaker, Loveman, and Stamatov 2004.

4. Brubaker 2009, 32.

5. On "national deixies," see Billig 1995.

6. Anderson 2006, 7.

7. See, for example, Seol and Skrentny 2009.

8. Schwenkel 2009, 6.

9. Lauenstein et al. 2015.

10. Malkki 1995.

11. Fox and Miller-Idriss 2008, 537.

12. Hearn and Antonsich 2018, 595.

13. Sunier, van der Linden, and van de Bovenkamp 2016.

14. P. Bui 2003.

15. People living in Germany must register their residency within two weeks of moving (*anmelden*) as well as before leaving Germany (*abmelden*). Individuals need a registration certificate (*Meldungbescheinigung*) to open a bank account, get a cell phone contract, and so forth.

16. See Barceló 2021 on how war might actually increase civic engagement in the long run.

17. D. Miller 1996, 413.

18. On how border crossers compare their context of reception with those facing their coethnics in other countries of resettlement, see Marrow 2013.

19. P. Bui 2003.

20. Jiménez 2010; Ochoa 2004.

21. Vega 2014.

22. I owe this and many more insights to conversations with Nguyễn-võ Thu-hương.

Chapter 5

1. Dalton and Weldon 2010, 11.

2. Fox and Miller Idriss 2008, 544.

3. L. Bui 2018, 1.

4. See Pfaff 2006 on insurgent versus reformist voice.

5. Aguilar-San Juan 2009; Brettell and Reed-Danahay 2011.

6. See Fox 2006.

7. Billig 1995.

8. Skey 2009.

9. Fox and Miller-Idriss 2008, 546.

10. Espiritu 2006, 2014.

11. Billig 2007, 309.

12. Skey 2008, 151.

13. Of course, there were competing Southern nationalist groups (Chapman 2013). But in postsocialist Berlin, people seldom acknowledged this.

14. P. T. Nguyen 2017.

15. Fox and Miller-Idriss 2008, 545.

16. Many respondents at times wove German or English into our conversations, even if they only knew a few words in these languages. As an international student who had passed the qualifying language exam, Hạnh could comfortably navigate German. Most of our conversations, however, were in Vietnamese.

17. Mausbach 2002, 79.

18. Although see Leshkowich on how this traditional Vietnamese dress "in fact has a relatively brief history marked throughout by significant foreign influence—first Chinese, then French and American" (2003, 81). In contrast with RfG, FaA did not enforce this as a dress code.

19. Leshkowich 2003, 97.

20. Fox and Miller-Idriss 2008, 546.

21. Billig 2017, 318.

22. Small 2012.

23. Billig 2017.

24. Fox and Miller-Idriss 2008.

25. P. Bui 2003.

Chapter 6

1. Foner and Alba 2008; Chen 2002.

2. Ebaugh and Chafetz 2000; Mora 2013; Herberg 1960.

3. Shams 2017.

4. Kurien 2001.

5. Ngo and Mai 2021, 122.

6. Glaeser 2000, 217.

7. See Ninh 2021 on how Vietnamese Catholics have melded their faith with refugee narratives of displacement.

8. Wimmer 2013, 204.

9. See Ngo and Mai 2021 for an overview of two eastern pagodas where, coincidentally, I also conducted fieldwork.

10. Glaeser 2000.

11. A separate study of Vietnamese Buddhists in Berlin found "that they liked to attend prayer and meditation led by South Vietnamese monks" (Ngo and Mai 2021, 114).

12. Lewis 2013.

13. Hüwelmeier 2013, 79–80.

14. Ibid.

15. P. V. Nguyen 2018, 748–749.

16. Fox and Miller-Idriss 2008.

17. Ngo and Mai 2021, 105.

18. Brody 1987, as cited in Ông and Meyer 2008.

19. A sangha is a Buddhist organization.

20. Historian Phi-Vân Nguyen, however, argues that "the Republic [of Vietnam] did not try to prioritize Catholicism over other faiths" (2018, 756).

21. Joiner 1964.

22. E. Miller 2013, 266.

23. However, see Ngo and Mai 2021 on controversy regarding Linh Thứu's self-proclaimed affiliation.

24. Soucy 2009.

25. Swenson 2020, 8.

26. Ironically, "being a Buddhist [in Vietnam in the 1950s] could not be reduced to nominal belonging to the faith. It implied a rigorous practice; greater discernment between legitimate, uncommitted Buddhists or those 'opposed to the faith'; and no concerns about the consequences of such mobilization" (P. V. Nguyen 2018, 759).

27. Others have similarly observed such tropes of brainwashed socialist citizens. These include studies of Cubans (Eckstein 2009), Germans (Glaeser 2000; Hogwood 2000), and Poles (Erdmans 1998), among others.

28. This assumption of how a Vietnamese woman should be socialized came up often, offering another dimension to how people perceive the north/south divide. One of my northern 1.5 generation interviewees, for example, remarked that she envied the children of southerners, who, she felt, had supposedly been raised with more gender-egalitarian attitudes. As her example, she cited my utter inability to cook and identify vegetables.

29. Historian David Hunt paints a similar portrait of ordinary Vietnamese people sitting at separate tables, leading separate lives even while living in the same village (2007, chap. 5). The schism there, however, was generational.

30. See, for example, Chen 2002; Kurien 2001.

31. Stein and Harel-Shalev 2017, 1986.

32. Glaeser 2000.

33. Brubaker 2015, 7.

Chapter 7

1. L. Bui 2018, 1.

2. Fox and Jones 2013, 391.

3. Brubaker and Cooper 2000.

4. Wimmer 2007, 28.

5. Fox and Jones 2013, 393.

6. Anderson 1992; Glick Schiller 2005.

7. Sheffer 2003.

8. K. Brown 2018, chap. 6.

9. Kim 2014.

10. I thank John O'Brien for this formulation.

11. Glaeser 2000.

12. Terence McCoy, "They Lost the Civil War and Fled to Brazil. Their Descendants Refuse to Take Down the Confederate Flag," *Washington Post*, July 12, 2020, https://www.washingtonpost.com/world/the_americas/brazil-confederate-flag-civil-war-americana-santa-barbara/2020/07/11/1e8a7c84-bec4-11ea-b4f6-cb39cd8940fb_story.html.

Appendix: Research Notes

1. Nagel 1998, 243.

2. Kibria 1993. The loss of South Vietnam presented not just South Vietnamese soldiers but also their American allies with a masculinity crisis (L. Bui 2018).

3. See Nagel 1998; Yuval-Davis 1993; Yuval-Davis and Anthias 1989.

4. See Foner 2009; Hondagneu-Sotelo 2000; Mahler and Pessar 2006; Pedraza 1991.

5. Increasingly, scholars are also training their lenses on transit sites, such as asylum and refugee camps, as well as locations in the Global South (Hamlin 2021; Lipman 2020).

6. Schwenkel 2014, 236.

7. Espiritu 2014.

8. Border crossings reveal not just the power of states to provide or deny protection but that states exercise disproportionate power relative to one another (Hamlin 2021; Lipman 2020).

9. Indeed, we should not assume a difference between internal and international migrants without investigating (Fitzgerald 2006). Because I did not include internal migrants in this study, however, I also do not want to assume similarities.

10. I thank Rosemary Byrne for pushing me to think about internal border crossings.

References

Aguilar-San Juan, Karin. 2009. *Little Saigons: Staying Vietnamese in America.* Minneapolis: University of Minnesota Press.

Anderson, Benedict. 1992. "Long-Distance Nationalism: World Capitalism and the Rise of Identity Politics." Wertham Lecture, Centre for Asian Studies Amsterdam.

———. 2006. *Imagined Communities,* rev. ed. London: Verso.

Arendt, Hannah. 1966. *The Origins of Totalitarianism,* 3rd ed. New York: Harcourt.

Barceló, Joan. 2021. "The Long-Term Effects of the Vietnam War on Civic Engagement." *Proceedings of the National Academy of Sciences* 118, no. 6, https://doi.org/10.1073/pnas.2015539118.

Beadle, Debbie, and Leah Davison. 2019. "Precarious Journeys: Mapping Vulnerabilities of Victims of Trafficking from Vietnam to Europe." London: ECPAT UK, Anti-Slavery International, and Pacific Links Foundation.

Bélanger, Danièle, and Khuât Thu Hông. 1996. "Marriage and the Family in Urban North Vietnam, 1965–1993." *Journal of Population* 2, no. 1: 83–112.

Besbris, Max, and Shamus Khan. 2017. "Less Theory. More Description." *Sociological Theory* 35, no. 2: 147–153.

Beuchling, Olaf. 2008. "'Manchmal schämt man sich für seine Landsleute . . .' Transnationale vietnamesische Verbrechensnetzwerke in Deutschland." *Südost-Asien* 4, no. 1: 84–87.

Billig, Michael. 1995. *Banal Nationalism.* Thousand Oaks, CA: Sage.

———. 2007. "Banal Nationalism and the Imagining of Politics." In *Everyday Nationhood: Theorising Culture, Identity, and Belonging after Banal Nationalism,* edited by Michael Skey and Marco Antonsich, 307–321. New York: Palgrave Macmillan.

Boot, Max. 2018. *The Road Not Taken: Edward Lansdale and the American Tragedy in Vietnam.* New York: Liverlight Publishing.

Borneman, John. 1992. State, Territory, and Identity Formation in the Postwar Berlins, 1945–1989. *Cultural Anthropology* 7, no. 1: 45–62.

Bösch, Frank. 2017. "Engagement für Flüchtlinge: Die Aufnahme vietnamesischer »Boat People« in der Bundesrepublik." *Zeithistorische Forschungen/ Studies in Contemporary History* 14, no. 1: 13–40.

Bösch, Frank, and Phi Hong Su. 2018. "Invisible, Successful, and Divided: Vietnamese in Germany since the Late 1970s." Forced Migration and Inequality Project Working Paper. Helsinki: United Nations University World Institute for Development Economics Research.

———. Forthcoming. "Competing Contexts of Reception in Refugee and Immigrant Incorporation: Vietnamese in West and East Germany." *Journal of Ethnic and Migration Studies.*

Brettell, Caroline B., and Deborah Reed-Danahay. 2011. *Civic Engagements: The Citizenship Practices of Indian and Vietnamese Immigrants.* Stanford, CA: Stanford University Press.

Breuilly, John. 1993. *Nationalism and the State,* 2nd ed. Manchester: Manchester University Press.

Brown, Karida L. 2018. *Gone Home: Race and Roots through Appalachia.* Chapel Hill: University of North Carolina Press.

Brown, Frederick Z. 1995. "Vietnam since the War (1975–1995)." *Wilson Quarterly* 19, no. 1: 64–87.

Brubaker, Rogers. 1992. *Citizenship and Nationhood in France and Germany.* Cambridge, MA: Harvard University Press.

———. 1996. *Nationalism Reframed: Nationhood and the National Question in the New Europe.* New York: Cambridge University Press.

———. 2009. "Ethnicity, Race, and Nationalism." *Annual Review of Sociology* 35, no. 1: 21–42.

———. 2015. "Religious Dimensions of Political Conflict and Violence." *Sociological Theory* 33, no. 1: 1–19.

Brubaker, Rogers, and Frederick Cooper. 2000. "Beyond 'identity.'" *Theory and Society* 29, no. 1: 1–47.

Brubaker, Rogers, and Jaeeun Kim. 2011. "Transborder Membership Politics in Germany and Korea." *European Journal of Sociology* 52, no. 1: 21–75.

Brubaker, Rogers, Mara Loveman, and Peter Stamatov. 2004. "Ethnicity as Cognition." *Theory and Society* 33, no. 1: 31–64.

Bui, Long. 2018. *Returns of War: South Vietnam and the Price of Refugee Memory.* New York: New York University Press.

Bui, Pipo. 2003. *Envisioning Vietnamese Migrants in Germany: Ethnic Stigma, Immigrant Origin Narratives, and Partial Masking.* Münster: Lit Verlag.

Calhoun, Craig. 1993. "Nationalism and Ethnicity." *Annual Review of Sociology* 19, no. 1: 211–239.

Chandra, Kanchan. 2006. "What Is Ethnic Identity and Does It Matter?" *Annual Review of Political Science* 9: 397–424.

———, ed. 2012. *Constructivist Theories of Ethnic Politics*. New York: Oxford University Press.

Chapman, Jessica M. 2013. *Cauldron of Resistance: Ngo Dinh Diem, the United States, and 1950s Southern Vietnam*. Ithaca, NY: Cornell University Press.

Chen, Carolyn. 2002. "The Religious Varieties of Ethnic Presence: A Comparison between a Taiwanese Immigrant Buddhist Temple and an Evangelical Christian Church." *Sociological of Religion* 63, no. 2: 215–238.

Choate, Mark I. 2008. *Emigrant Nation: The Making of Italy Abroad*. Cambridge, MA: Harvard University Press.

Cisneros, Josue David. 2013. *The Border Crossed Us: Rhetorics of Borders, Citizenship, and Latina/o Identity*. Tuscaloosa: University of Alabama Press.

Cook-Martín, David. 2019. "Temp Nations? A Research Agenda on Migration, Temporariness, and Membership." *American Behavioral Scientist* 63, no. 9: 1389–1403.

Coutin, Susan Bibler. 2007. *Nations of Emigrants: Shifting Boundaries of Citizenship in El Salvador and the United States*. Ithaca, NY: Cornell University Press.

Dalton, Russell J., and Steven Weldon. 2010. "Germans Divided? Political Culture in a United Germany." *German Politics* 19, no. 1: 9–23.

Del Real, Deisy. 2019. "Toxic Ties: The Reproduction of Legal Violence within Mixed-Status Intimate Partners, Relatives, and Friends." *International Migration Review* 53, no. 2: 548–570.

Dennis, Mike. 2005. "Die vietnamesischen Vertragsarbeiter und Vertragsarbeiterinnen in der DDR, 1980–1989." In *Erfolg in der Nische? Die Vietnamesen in der DDR und in Ostdeutschland*, edited by Karen Weiss and Mike Dennis, 15–49. Münster: Lit Verlag.

———. 2007. "Working under Hammer and Sickle: Vietnamese Workers in the German Democratic Republic, 1980–89." *German Politics* 16, no. 3: 339–357.

———. 2017. "Arbeiten in einem kommunistischen 'Paradies.' Vietnamesische Migration in den 1980er Jahren." In *UnSichtbar. Vietnamesisch-Deutsche Wirklichkeiten*, edited by Bengü Kocatürk-Schuster et al., 78–97. Bonn: Documentation Center and Museum of Migration in Germany and Friedrich Ebert Foundation.

Dreby, Joanna. 2010. *Divided by Borders: Mexican Migrants and Their Children*. Berkeley: University of California Press.

Dror, Olga. 2018. *Making Two Vietnams: War and Youth Identities, 1965–1975*. Cambridge: Cambridge University Press.

Ebaugh, Helen Rose, and Janet Saltzman Chafetz. 2000. *Religion and the New*

Immigrants: Continuities and Adaptations in Immigrant Congregations.
  Walnut Creek, CA: AltaMira Press.
Eckstein, Susan Eva. 2009. *The Immigrant Divide: How Cuban Americans
  Changed the US and Their Homeland.* New York: Routledge.
Elsner, Eva-Maria, and Lothar Elsner. 1992. "Ausländer und *Ausländerpolitik*
  in der *DDR.*" In *Zwischen Nationalstaat und multikultureller Gesellschaft.
  Einwanderung und Fremdenfeindlichkeit in der Bundesrepublik Deutsch-
  land,* edited by Manfred Heßler, 185–209. Berlin: Gesellschaftswissen-
  schaftliches Forum.
Erdmans, Mary Patrice. 1998. *Opposite Poles: Immigrants and Ethnics in Polish
  Chicago, 1976–1990.* University Park: Pennsylvania State University Press.
Espiritu, Yen Le. 1993. *Asian American Panethnicity: Bridging Institutions and
  Identities.* Philadelphia: Temple University Press.
———. "The 'We-Win-Even-When-We-Lose' Syndrome: U.S. Press Coverage
  of the Twenty-Fifth Anniversary of the 'Fall of Saigon.'" *American Quar-
  terly* 58, no. 2: 329–352.
———. 2014. *Body Counts: The Vietnam War and Militarized Refuge(e).* Berke-
  ley: University of California Press.
Fall, Bernard B. 1967. *Last Reflections on a War.* Garden City, NY: Doubleday.
Fitzgerald, David. 2006. "Towards a Theoretical Ethnography of Migration."
  Qualitative Sociology 29, no. 1: 1–24.
———. 2008. *A Nation of Emigrants: How Mexico Manages Its Migration.*
  Berkeley: University of California Press.
———. 2019. *Refuge beyond Reach: How Rich Democracies Repel Asylum Seek-
  ers.* Oxford: Oxford University Press.
FitzGerald, David Scott, and Rawan Arar. 2018. "The Sociology of Refugee
  Migration." *Annual Review of Sociology* 44, no. 1: 387–406.
Foner, Nancy. 2009. "Gender and Migration: West Indians in Comparative
  Perspective." *International Migration* 47, no. 1: 3–29.
Foner, Nancy, and Richard Alba. 2008. "Immigrant Religion in the U.S. and
  Western Europe: Bridge or Barrier to Inclusion?" *International Migration
  Review* 42, no. 2: 360–392.
Fox, Jon E. 2003. "National Identities on the Move: Transylvanian Hungarian
  Labour Migrants in Hungary." *Journal of Ethnic and Migration Studies* 29,
  no. 3: 449–466.
———. 2006. "Consuming the Nation: Holidays, Sports, and the Production
  of Collective Belonging." *Ethnic and Racial Studies* 29, no. 2: 217–236.
Fox, Jon E., and Demelza Jones. "Migration, Everyday Life and the Ethnicity
  Bias." *Ethnicities* 13, no. 4: 385–400.
Fox, Jon E., and Cynthia Miller-Idriss. 2008. "Everyday Nationhood." *Ethnicities* 8, no. 4: 536–576.

Gao, Jia. 2006. "Organized International Asylum-Seeker Networks: Formation and Utilization by Chinese Students." *International Migration Review*
40, no. 2: 294–317.

Gellner, Ernest. 2006. *Nations and Nationalisms*, 2nd ed. Ithaca, NY: Cornell
University Press.

Glaeser, Andreas. 2000. *Divided in Unity: Identity, Germany, and the Berlin
Police*. Chicago: University of Chicago Press.

Glick Schiller, Nina. 2005. "Long-Distance Nationalism." In *Encyclopedia of
Diasporas*, edited by Melvin Ember, Carol R. Ember, and Ian Skoggard.
New York: Springer.

Glick Schiller, Nina, Linda Basch, and Cristina Szanton Blanc. 1995. "From
Immigrant to Transmigrant: Theorizing Transnational Migration." *An-
thropological Quarterly* 68, no. 1: 48–63.

Gordon, Milton M. 1964. *Assimilation in American Life: The Role of Race, Religion, and National Origins*. New York: Oxford University Press.

Graziano, Manlio. 2017. *What Is a Border?* Stanford, CA: Stanford University
Press.

Green, Simon. 2001. "Immigration, Asylum and Citizenship in Germany: The
Impact of Unification on the German Republic." *West European Politics*
24, no. 4: 82–104.

Ha, Noa. 2015. "Handel(n) und Wandel(n): Urbane Informalität, städtische
Repräsentation und Migrantische Existenzsicherung in Berlin am Beispiel
des mobilen Straßenhandel." PhD diss., Technical University Berlin.

Haddad, Emma. 2008. *The Refugee in International Society: Between Sover-
eigns*. Cambridge: Cambridge University Press.

Hagan, Jacqueline Maria. 1994. *Deciding to Be Legal: A Maya Community in
Houston*. Philadelphia: Temple University Press.

Hailbronner, Kay. 1994. "Asylum Law Reform in the German Constitution."
American University International Law Review 9, no. 4: 159–179.

Hamlin, Rebecca. 2012. "International Law and Administrative Insulation:
A Comparison of Refugee Status Determination Regimes in the United
States, Canada, and Australia." *Law and Social Inquiry* 37, no. 4: 933–968.

———. 2021. *Crossing: How We Label and React to People on the Move*. Stanford, CA: Stanford University Press.

Hamlin, Rebecca, and Philip E. Wolgin. 2012. "Symbolic Politics and Policy
Feedback: The United Nations Protocol Relating to the Status of Refugees
and American Refugee Policy in the Cold War." *International Migration
Review* 46, no. 3: 586–624.

Hansen, Peter. 2009. "Bắc Di Cư: Catholic Refugees from the North of Vietnam, and Their Role in the Southern Republic, 1954–1959." *Journal of Vietnamese Studies* 4, no. 3: 173–211.

Hardy, Andrew. 2001. "Rules and Resources: Negotiating the Household Registration System in Vietnam under Reform." *Sojourn* 16, no. 2: 187–212.

Hearn, Jonathan, and Marco Antonsich. 2018. "Theoretical and Methodological Considerations for the Study of Banal and Everyday Nationalism." *Nations and Nationalism* 24, no. 3: 594–605.

Herberg, Will. 1960. *Protestant—Catholic—Jew: An Essay in American Religious Sociology*. Chicago: University of Chicago Press.

Hernández-León, Rubén. 2008. *Metropolitan Migrants: The Migration of Urban Mexicans to the United States*. Berkeley: University of California Press.

Hillmann, Felicitas. 2005. "Riders on the Storm: Vietnamese in Germany's Two Migration Systems." In *Asian Migrants and European Labour Markets: Patterns and Processes of Immigrant Labour Market Insertion in Europe*, edited by Ernst Spaan, Felicitas Hillmann, and Ton van Naerssen, 80–100. New York: Routledge.

Hobsbawn, Eric, and Terence Ranger. 1983. *The Invention of Tradition*. Cambridge: Cambridge University Press.

Hogwood, Patricia. 2000. "After the GDR: Reconstructing Identity in Post-Communist Germany." *Journal of Communist Studies and Transition Politics* 16, no. 4: 45–67.

Hondagneu-Sotelo, Pierrette. 2000. "Feminism and Migration." *Annals of the American Academy of Political and Social Science* 571, no. 1: 107–120.

Hunt, David. 2007. *Vietnam's Southern Revolution: From Peasant Insurrection to Total War*. Amherst: University of Massachusetts Press.

Hüwelmeier, Gertrud. 2013. "Bazaar Pagodas—Transnational Religion, Postsocialist Marketplaces and Vietnamese Migrant Women in Berlin." *Religion and Gender* 3, no. 1: 76–89.

Jiménez, Tomás R. 2010. *Replenished Ethnicity : Mexican Americans, Immigration, and Identity*. Berkeley: University of California Press.

Joiner, Charles A. 1964. "South Vietnam's Buddhist Crisis: Organization for Charity, Dissidence, and Unity." *Asian Survey* 4, no. 7: 915–928.

Itzigsohn, José, and Silvia Giorguli Saucedo. 2002. "Immigrant Incorporation and Sociocultural Transnationalism." *International Migration Review* 36, no. 3: 766–798.

Keating, Joshua. 2018. *Invisible Countries: Journeys to the Edge of Nationhood*. New Haven, CT: Yale University Press.

Keith, Charles. 2012. *Catholic Vietnam: A Church from Empire to Nation*. Berkeley: University of California Press.

Kibria, Nazli. 1993. *Family Tightrope: The Changing Lives of Vietnamese Americans*. Princeton, NJ: Princeton University Press.

Kim, Jaeeun. 2014. "The Colonial State, Migration, and Diasporic Nationhood in Korea." *Comparative Studies in Society and History* 56, no. 1: 34–66.

———. 2016. *Contested Embrace: Transborder Membership Politics in Twentieth-Century Korea*. Stanford, CA: Stanford University Press.

Klessmann, Maria. 2011. "'Wohnen-Arbeiten.' Zu den Wohnbedingungen vietnamesischer Vertragsarbeiter in Ost-Berlin." In *Transit. Transfer. Politik und Praxis der Einwanderung in die DDR 1945–1990*, edited by Kim Christian Priemel, 192–210. Berlin: Bebra.

Kligman, Gail, and Katherine Verdery. 2011. *Peasants under Siege: The Collectivization of Romanian Agriculture, 1949–1962*. Princeton, NJ: Princeton University Press.

Klusmeyer, Douglas B. 1993. "Aliens, Immigrants, and Citizens: The Politics of Inclusion in the Federal Republic of Germany." *Daedalus* 122, no. 3: 81–114.

Kocatürk-Schuster, Bengü, Arnd Kolb, Thanh Long, Günther Schultze, and Sascha Wölck, eds. 2017. *UnSichtbar: Vietnamesisch-Deutsche Wirklichkeiten*. Bonn: Documentation Center and Museum of Migration in Germany and Friedrich Ebert Foundation.

Kolinsky, Eva. 2004. "Former Contract Workers from Vietnam in Germany between State Socialism and Democracy, 1989–1993." *German as a Foreign Language* 3, no. 1: 83–101.

Korntheuer, Annette, Paul Pritchard, and Débora B. Maehler, eds. 2017. *Structural Context of Refugee Integration in Canada and Germany*. Leibniz: GESIS Leibniz Institute for Social Sciences.

Kurien, Prema. 2001. "Religion, Ethnicity and Politics: Hindu and Muslim Indian Immigrants in the United States." *Ethnic and Racial Studies* 24, no. 2: 263–293.

Kwon, Heonik. 2010. *The Other Cold War*. New York: Columbia University Press.

Laitin, David D. 1998. *Identity in Formation: The Russian-Speaking Populations in the Near Abroad*. Ithaca, NY: Cornell University Press.

Lauenstein, Oliver, Jeffrey S. Murer, Margarete Boos, and Stephen Reicher. 2015. "'Oh Motherland I Pledge to Thee . . .': A Study into Nationalism, Gender and the Representation of an Imagined Family Within National Anthems." *Nations and Nationalism* 21, no. 2: 309–329.

Le, Loan Kieu, and Phi Hong Su. 2018. "Party Identification and the Immigrant Cohort Hypothesis: The Case of Vietnamese Americans." *Politics, Groups, and Identities* 6, no. 4: 743–763.

Leshkowich, Ann Marie. 2003. "The Ao Dai Goes Global: How International Influences and Female Entrepreneurs Have Shaped Vietnam's 'National Costume.'" In *Re-Orienting Fashion: The Globalization of Asian Dress*, edited by Sandra Niessen, Ann Marie Leshkowich, and Carla Jones, 79–115. New York: Bloomsbury.

———. 2014. "Standardized Forms of Vietnamese Selfhood: An Ethnographic Genealogy of Documentation." *American Ethnologist* 41, no. 1: 143–162.

Lewis, James F. 2013. "Vietnamese Religions, Asian Studies, and the Rule of Law." *Review of Faith and International Affairs* 11, no. 2: 55–63.

Lipman, Jana K. 2020. *In Camps: Vietnamese Refugees, Asylum Seekers, and Repatriates*. Oakland: University of California Press.

Loescher, Gil, and John Allen Scanlan. 1986. *Calculated Kindness: Refugees and America's Half-Open Door, 1945 to the Present*. New York: Free Press.

Mahler, Sarah J., and Patricia R. Pessar. 2006. "Gender Matters: Ethnographers Bring Gender from the Periphery toward the Core of Migration Studies." *International Migration Review* 40, no. 1: 27–63.

Malešević, Siniša. 2019. *Grounded Nationalisms: A Sociological Analysis*. Cambridge: Cambridge University Press.

Malkki, Liisa H. 1995. *Purity and Exile: Violence, Memory, and National Cosmology among Hutu Refugees in Tanzania*. Chicago: University of Chicago Press.

Marr, David G. 2004. "A Brief History of Local Government in Vietnam." In *Beyond Hanoi: Local Government in Vietnam*, edited by Benedict J. Tria Kerkvliet and David G. Marr, 28–53. Singapore: Institute of Southeast Asian Studies.

Marrow, Helen B. 2013. "In Ireland 'Latin Americans Are Kind of Cool': Evaluating a National Context of Reception with a Transnational Lens." *Ethnicities* 13, no. 5: 645–666.

Mausbach, Wilfried. 2002. "European Perspectives on the War in Vietnam." *German Historical Institute Bulletin* 30, no. 1: 71–86.

Mehrländer, Ursula, Casten Ascheberg, and Jörg Ueltzhöffer. 1996. *Situation der Ausländischen Arbeitnehmer und Ihrer Familienangehörigen in der Bundesrepublik Deutschland*. Berlin: Sozialwissenschaftliches Institut der Friedrich Ebert Stiftung.

Menjívar, Cecilia. 2006. "Liminal Legality: Salvadoran and Guatemalan Immigrants' Lives in the United States." *American Journal of Sociology* 111, no. 4: 999–1037.

Metzner, Edward P., Huynh Van Chinh, Chan Van Phuc, and Le Nguyen Binh. 2001. *Reeducation in Postwar Vietnam: Personal Postscripts to Peace*. College Station: Texas A&M University.

Meyer, Birgit. "Mobilizing Theory: Concluding Thoughts." In *Refugees and Religion*, edited by Birgit Meyer and Peter van der Veer, 256–273. London: Bloomsbury Academic.

Miller, David. 1996. "On Nationality." *Nations and Nationalism* 2, no. 3: 409–421.

Miller, Edward. 2013. *Misalliance: Ngo Dinh Diem, the United States, and the Fate of South Vietnam*. Cambridge, MA: Harvard University Press.

Moise, Edwin E. 1976. "Land Reform and Land Reform Errors in North Vietnam." *Pacific Affairs* 49, no. 1: 70–92.

Mora, G. Cristina. 2013. "Religion and the Organizational Context of Immigrant Civic Engagement: Mexican Catholicism in the USA." *Ethnic and Racial Studies* 36, no. 11: 1647–1665.

Nagel, Joane. 1998. "Masculinity and Nationalism: Gender and Sexuality in the Making of Nations." *Ethnic and Racial Studies* 21, no. 2: 242–269.

Ngo, Tam T. T., and Nga T. Mai. 2021. "In Search of a Vietnamese Buddhist Space in Germany." In *Refugees and Religion*, edited by Birgit Meyer and Peter van der Veer, 105–122. London: Bloomsbury Academic.

Nguyen, Mimi Thi. 2012. *The Gift of Freedom: War, Debt, and Other Refugee Passages*. Durham, NC: Duke University Press.

Nguyen, Phi-Vân. 2016. "Fighting the First Indochina War Again? Catholic Refugees in South Vietnam, 1954–59." *Sojourn: Journal of Social Issues in Southeast Asia* 31, no. 1: 207–246.

Nguyen, Phuong Tran. 2017. *Becoming Refugee American: The Politics of Rescue in Little Saigon*. Urbana: University of Illinois Press.

Nguyễn Thị Điểu. 2019. "'A Day in the Life': Nation-Building the Republic of Ngô Đình Diệm, 26 October 1956, Symbolically." *Modern Asian Studies* 53, no. 2: 718–753.

Ninh, Thien-Huong. 2021. "The Virgin Mary Became Asian: Diasporic Nationalism among Vietnamese Catholic Refugees in the United States and Germany." In *Refugees and Religion*, edited by Birgit Meyer and Peter van der Veer, 68–86. London: Bloomsbury Academic.

Ochoa, Gilda L. 2004. *Becoming Neighbors in a Mexican American Community: Power, Conflict, and Solidarity*. Austin: University of Texas Press.

Ogbu, John U. 1987. "Variability in Minority School Performance: A Problem in Search of an Explanation." *Anthropology and Education Quarterly* 18, no. 4: 312–334.

Okamoto, Dina, and G. Cristina Mora. 2014. "Panethnicity." *Annual Review of Sociology* 40: 219–239.

Ông, Như-Ngọc T., and David S. Meyer. 2008. "Protest and Political Incorporation: Vietnamese American Protests in Orange County, California, 1975–2001." *Journal of Vietnamese Studies* 3, no. 1: 78–107.

Pedraza, Silvia. 1991. "Women and Migration: The Social Consequences of Gender." *Annual Review of Sociology* 17: 303–325.

———. 2007. *Political Disaffection in Cuba's Revolution and Exodus*. Cambridge: Cambridge University Press.

Pfaff, Steven. 2006. *Exit-Voice Dynamics and the Collapse of East Germany: The Crisis of Leninism and the Revolution of 1989*. Durham, NC: Duke University Press.

Pike, Douglas. 1981. "Vietnam in 1980: The Gathering Storm." *Asian Survey* 21, no. 1: 84–92.

Pinkel, Sheila. 2010. "The Value of Transnational Analysis," *Trans Asia Photography Review* 1, no. 1, https://quod.lib.umich.edu/t/tap/7977573.0001.102/-why-asian-photography?trgt=div1_pinkel;view=fulltext.

Portes, Alejandro, and József Böröcz. 1989. "Contemporary Immigration: Theoretical Perspectives on Its Determinants and Modes of Incorporation." *International Migration Review* 23, no. 3: 606–630.

Portes, Alejandro, and Rubén G. Rumbaut. 2014. *Immigrant America: A Portrait*, rev. ed. Berkeley: University of California Press.

Sammartino, Annemarie H. 2010. *The Impossible Border: Germany and the East, 1914–1922*. Ithaca, NY: Cornell University Press.

Schönwälder, Karen. 2004. "Why Germany's Guestworkers Were Largely Europeans: The Selective Principles of Post-War Labour Recruitment Policy." *Ethnic and Racial Studies* 27, no. 2: 248–265.

Schwenkel, Christina. 2009. *The American War in Contemporary Vietnam: Transnational Remembrance and Representation*. Bloomington: Indiana University Press.

———. 2014. "Rethinking Asian Mobilities: Socialist Migration and Post-Socialist Repatriation of Vietnamese Contract Workers in Germany." *Critical Asian Studies* 46, no. 2: 235–258.

———. 2015. "Socialist Mobilities: Crossing New Terrains in Vietnamese Migration Histories." *Central and Eastern European Migration Review* 4, no. 1: 1–13.

Seol, Dong-Hoon, and John D. Skrentny. 2009. "Ethnic Return Migration and Hierarchical Nationhood: Korean Chinese Foreign Workers in South Korea." *Ethnicities* 9, no. 2: 147–174.

Shacknove, Andrew E. 1985. "Who Is a Refugee?" *Ethnics* 95, no. 2: 274–284.

Shams, Tahseen. 2017. "Mirrored Boundaries: How Ongoing Homeland-Hostland Contexts Shape Bangladeshi Immigrant Collective Identity Formation." *Ethnic and Racial Studies* 40, no. 4: 713–731.

———. 2020. *Here, There, and Elsewhere: The Making of Immigrant Identities in a Globalized World*. Stanford, CA: Stanford University Press.

Sheffer, Gabriel. 2003. *Diaspora Politics: At Home Abroad*. Cambridge: Cambridge University Press.

Shevchenko, Olga. 2015. "Resisting Resistance: Everyday Life, Practical Competence, and Neoliberal Rhetoric in Postsocialist Russia." In *Everyday Life in Russia: Past and Present*, edited by Choi Chatterjee et al., 52–71. Bloomington: Indiana University Press.

Skey, Michael. 2008. "'Carnivals of Surplus Emotion?' Towards an Understanding of the Significance of Ecstatic Nationalism in a Globalising World." *Studies in Ethnicity and Nationalism* 6, no. 2: 143–161.

———. 2009. "The National in Everyday Life: A Critical Engagement with Michael Billig's Thesis of *Banal Nationalism*." *Sociological Review* 57, no. 2: 331–346.

Słowiak, Jarema. 2019. "The Role of the International Commission for Supervision and Control in Vietnam in the Population Exchange between Vietnamese States during Years 1954–1955." *Prace Historyczne* 146, no. 3: 621–634.

Small, Ivan V. 2012. "'Over There': Imaginative Displacements in Vietnamese Remittance Gift Economies." *Journal of Vietnamese Studies* 7, no. 3: 157–183.

Smith, Anthony D. 1986. *The Ethnic Origins of Nations*. Malden, MA: Blackwell.

Smith, Robert Courtney. 2006. *Mexican New York: Transnational Lives of New Immigrants*. Berkeley: University of California Press.

Soucy, Alexander. 2009. "Language, Orthodoxy, and Performances of Authority in Vietnamese Buddhism." *Journal of the American Academy of Religion* 77, no. 2: 348–371.

Spener, David. 2009. *Clandestine Crossings: Migrants and Coyotes on the Texas-Mexico Border*. Ithaca, NY: Cornell University Press.

Stein, Arthur A., and Ayelet Harel-Shalev. 2017. "Ancestral and Instrumental in the Politics of Ethnic and Religious Conflict." *Ethnic and Racial Studies* 40, no. 12: 1981–2000.

Stepick, Alex, and Carol Dutton Stepick. 2009. "Diverse Contexts of Reception and Feelings of Belonging." *Forum: Qualitative Social Research* 10, no. 3: 1–19.

Sunier, Thijl, Helen van der Linden, and Ellen van de Bovenkamp. 2016. "The Long Arm of the State? Transnationalism, Islam, and Nation-Building: The Case of Turkey and Morocco." *Contemporary Islam* 10: 401–420.

Surak, Kristin. 2012. *Making Tea, Making Japan: Cultural Nationalism in Practice*. Stanford, CA: Stanford University Press.

———. 2013. "Guestworkers: A Taxonomy." *New Left Review* 84, no. 3: 84–102.

———. 2017. "Migration Industries and the State: Guestwork Programs in East Asia." *International Migration Review* 52, no. 2: 487–523.

Swenson, Sara Ann. 2020. "Compassion without Pity: Buddhist *dāna* as Charity, Humanitarianism, and Altruism." *Religion Compass* 14, no. 9: e12371.

Taylor, K. W. 2013. *A History of the Vietnamese*. New York: Cambridge University Press.

Toai, Doan Van. 1980. *Der Vietnamesische Gulag*. Köln: Kiepenheuer & Witsch.

Trân Thi Liên. 2005. "The Catholic Question in North Vietnam: From Polish Sources, 1954–56." *Cold War History* 5, no. 4: 427–449.

Triadafilopoulous, Triadafilos, and Karen Schönwälder. 2006. "How the Federal Republic Became an Immigration Country: Norms, Politics and the Failure of West Germany's Guest Worker System." *German Politics and Society* 24, no. 3: 1–19.

United Nations High Commissioner for Refugees. 2000. "Flight from Indochina." In *The State of the World's Refugees 2000: Fifty Years of Humanitarian Action*, chap. 4. Geneva: UNHCR.

Valverde, Kieu Linh Caroline. 2003. "Making Vietnamese Music Transnational: Sounds of Home, Resistance and Change." *Amerasia Journal* 29, no. 1: 29–49.

———. 2012. *Transnationalizing Viet Nam: Community, Culture, and Politics in the Diaspora*. Philadelphia: Temple University Press.

Vega, Irene I. 2014. "Conservative Rationales, Racial Boundaries: A Case Study of Restrictionist Mexican Americans." *American Behavioral Scientist* 58, no. 13: 1764–1783.

Verdery, Katherine. 1993. "Whither 'Nation' and 'Nationalism?'" *Daedalus* 122, no. 3: 37–46.

VLab Berlin. 2020. *Ist Zuhause da, wo die Sternfrüchte süß sind?* Berlin: VLab.

Waldinger, Roger. 2015. *The Cross-Border Connection: Immigrants, Emigrants, and Their Homelands*. Cambridge, MA: Harvard University Press.

Weiss, Karin. 2005. "Nach der Wende: Vietnamesische Vertragsarbeiter und Vertragsarbeiterinnen in Ostdeutschland Heute." In *Erfolg in der Nische? Die Vietnamesen in der DDR und in Ostdeutschland*, edited by Karin Weiss and Mike Dennis. Münster: Lit Verlag.

Wimmer, Andreas. 2007. "How (Not) to Think about Ethnicity in Immigrant Societies: A Boundary Making Perspective." Policy and Society Working Paper 44. Oxford: University of Oxford ESRC Centre on Migration,

———. 2008. "The Making and Unmaking of Ethnic Boundaries: A Multilevel Process Theory." *American Journal of Sociology* 113, no. 4: 970–1022.

———. 2013. *Ethnic Boundary Making: Institutions, Power, Networks*. New York: Oxford University Press.

Wolf, Bernd. 2007. "The Vietnamese Diaspora in Germany: Structure and Potentials for Cooperation with a Focus on Berlin and Hesse." Eschborn: Deutsche Gesellschaft für Technische Zusammenarbeit GmbH.

Woodside, Alexander. 1970. "Decolonization and Agricultural Reform in Northern Vietnam." *Asian Survey* 10, no. 8: 705–723.

Young, Marilyn B. 1991. *The Vietnam Wars, 1945–1990.* New York: HarperCollins.

Yuval-Davis, Nira. 1993. "Gender and Nation." *Ethnic and Racial Studies* 16, no. 4: 621–632.

Yuval-Davis, Nira, and Floya Anthias, eds. 1989. *Woman-Nation-State.* Basingstoke, UK: Macmillan.

Zhou, Min, and Carl L. Bankston. 1998. *Growing Up American: How Vietnamese Children Adapt to Life in the United States.* New York: Russell Sage Foundation.

Zolberg, Aristide R. 1983. "The Formation of New States as a Refugee-Generating Process." *Annals of the American Academy of Political and Social Science* 467, no. 1: 24–38.

Index

Note: Page numbers in *italics* indicate illustrative material.

racism and xenophobia, 56, 67–68
reeducation camps, x, 13, 41, 43,
    44–45
refugees: and citizen-state-territory
    nexus, 18; contract workers,
    converging life outcomes with,
    72; contract workers, solidar-
    ity with vs. prejudice against,
    10–11, 64–67; vs. contract work-
    ers' frame of reference, 60–63,
    62; escape by boat, 3, 50, 56,
    57, 168nn1–3; in ethnic na-
    tion ranking, 76, 78, 86, 87, 88;
    general oppression vs. targeted
    persecution, 45–46; as label
    for southern and anticom-
    munist allegiance, 10, 73; and
    migrant/refugee binary, 6, 10,
    52–53; recognition of northern
    Vietnamese as, 52, 168–69n7; re-
    settlement estimates, 69, 170n55;
    South Vietnamese international
    students as, 43; West Germany's
    reception of, 50–51, 54–58, 55, 57
Refugees for Germany. See RfG
religion. See Buddhism; Catholics
Republic of Vietnam. See RVN
return travel, 107–9
RfG (Refugees for Germany): anti-
    communist rhetoric in, 102–3,
    106–9, 111–13, 114–15; demograph-
    ics, 93; expressions of national-
    ism, 101–2, 104–6, 109–10, 111;
    gatekeeping, 113–14, 115, 116
RVN (Republic of Vietnam; South
    Vietnam): citizens punished
    for disloyalty, 41–42; citizens
    rewarded for loyalty, 40–41; citi-
    zens' understanding of the war,
    42; establishment, 1, 28, 164n1;
    map, 2; migration of northern-
    ers to, 32–34; religion in, 33, 128,

173n20; state formation process,
    overview, 30–31

Saigon (Hồ Chí Minh City), 3, 94, 95,
    99
Sáu (pseudonym), 98
Schubert, Sebastian, xi
second-generation Vietnamese
    Germans, 136–38, 160–61
sexualized stereotypes, 66
Socialist Republic of Vietnam. See
    Vietnam
social networks. See coethnic
    networks
Sơn (pseudonym), 38–39, 124–25,
    139–40
south/north divide. See Buddhism;
    coethnic networks; contract
    workers; DRV; ethnic nation-
    hood, ranking of; refugees; RVN
South Vietnam. See RVN
state formation: as border crossing,
    6–7; and citizen-state-territory
    nexus, 16–19; and nation build-
    ing, 30–31
students abroad: Chinese Student
    Protection Act (U.S., 1992), 167–
    68n68; impacted by Vietnam re-
    unification, 43, 57; scholarships,
    37, 40
symbols, national, 98, 99–102, 104–6,
    109–10, 111, 124–25

Tài (pseudonym): author's intro-
    duction to, 20; identification as
    southerner, 34; migration to Ger-
    many, 3–5; migration to RVN,
    1–3, 33; view of contract workers
    and northerners, 10–11, 114–15
Thailand and Thais, 3, 50, 168n1
Thẩm (pseudonym), 64, 65–66, 121
Thích Quang Đức, 128

CPSIA information can be obtained
at www.ICGtesting.com
Printed in the USA
JSHW041515181221
21240JS00007B/9